The Single Parent Experience

*Impressions & Perceptions -
Written With Love*

by

Julie Ruth Jayson

*BA (Hons) Theology, PGCE –PCE Adult Literacy,
MA Edu. (Learning & Teaching), Cert. TEFL (UK)*

RB

Rossendale Books

Published by Lulu Enterprises Inc.

3101 Hillsborough Street

Suite 210

Raleigh, NC 27607-5436

United States of America

Published in paperback 2013

Copyright Julie Ruth Jayson © 2013

ISBN : 978-1-291-56102-9

All rights reserved, Copyright under Berne Copyright Convention and Pan American Convention. No part of this book may be reproduced, stored in a retrieval system, or transmitted in any form or by any means, electronic, mechanical, photocopying, recording or otherwise, without prior permission of the author. The author's moral rights have been asserted.

*"Take responsibility for the place you hold here.
The person you were meant to be,
The gift you were meant to give,
Nobody can take that away from you"*

Oprah Winfrey
The Master Class - Super Soul Sunday (OWN)

Contents

Dedication 7

Foreword.. 10

Chapter One   What is Single Parenting? 23

Chapter Two   Causes of Single Parenting? 64

Chapter Three   Myths About Single Parenting 77

Chapter Four   What Children Need 81

Chapter Five   Questions to Jog Your Memory and Get You Started on Something Worthwhile 82

Chapter Six   Common Struggles of Single Parents 89

Chapter Seven   Fatherless Boys Raised by Mothers 92

Chapter Eight   Questions That Children Ask: How to Respond 99

Chapter Nine   Single Mothers By Choice 103

Chapter Ten   How Does Single Parenting Affect Children? 111

Chapter Eleven   Starting Another Relationship As a Single Parent 116

Chapter Twelve   Blended Families 126

Chapter Thirteen   Advantages of Children With Two Parents 129

Chapter Fourteen   Balancing the Role of Parenting 131

Chapter Fifteen   Single Parent Statistics....... 145

Chapter Sixteen   Single Parenting Quotes ... 150

Chapter Seventeen   Famous People Raised by Single Mothers 155

Online Help For Single Parents..................... 158

Dedication

With all my affection, I dedicate this book to my dearest and most adorable son, Alvin Mark Jayson without whom it would not have been possible for me to be where I am and have the courage to write this precious book. He has given me incredible joy and happiness that I never experienced as a child but am now enjoying as a mother. He is such a priceless gift and treasure from God. I could never have prayed for anything better. He constantly puts a smile on my face and he is a bundle of joy, he brings warmth into my heart, he has made me realize who I was meant to be. He holds my hand and he is a shoulder for me to lean on. He makes my life complete. I could never achieve anything better than being a mother and being called "Mum" as he addresses me. I cherish every moment we spend together. I have seen him grow from a tiny tender toddler into a young personable teenager. The journey has not been easy for both of us, but we have managed to walk under the grace, divine protection, divine provision, divine guidance of our loving God amidst all these challenges. His sole presence overshadows us constantly.

My greatest appreciation is to God who has made my life and Alvin's a possibility and *part of mankind. He is our everything and we are completely secure in Him alone. This book is also a tribute to my own mother whom I longed for all my life to be around for me as a little girl, as a budding teenager and through to this moment as a grown up, but life's circumstances denied me that. I appreciate the fact that I have been able to be around my own son constantly loving, and constantly safeguarding him in every way, watching his every step and smiles and tantrums. It's a tribute to my own father that I will never know who he was and to where he vanished. This book is an accolade to Alvin's dad who fathered him and he misses him so dearly wishing he was around to see him grow and hold his hand as father and son.*

A huge sincere gratitude to the most loving Nganwa family that supported me for years when I needed a home to grow and you opened your doors and embraced me. Your family values shaped me into the self-driven and ambitious individual that I have become. I became part of your family. You and your adorable children with whom I grew up together remain my role models.

A huge thank you to all those loving and selfless individuals whom God specifically and prophetically brought along our path to love us unconditionally, and be there for us constantly all the way through, such as

Edmund Bannerman and his dear family, a true man of God with the big loving heart of a father, he remains an embodiment of practical Christianity and what Christians should do. Theresa Francis, whom we call our dear golden, angel mother, her love is priceless to us. Lucy, Olive, Peace and Susan, my best friends, you gave everything you could to Alvin and I. You were constantly there when we needed you most. To Helen, for her professional support. My deepest thanks also goes to all those who share joy with us along the way including the members of West Bromwich Community Church (WBCC) who are our spiritual and faith family. God bless you all.

Viva! Viva! To all Single Mothers and Single Fathers out there.

Foreword

Being a parent is one of the greatest gifts on earth that God has bestowed on mankind. Marriage brings happiness and fullness of joy into our lives provided we make it work regardless of its own challenges and when children are part of the marriage, we can never desire anything better and fulfilling. Being a single parent can be one of the most challenging moments in life, but delightful and equally rewarding so long as we embrace it and give it our best. Whichever way, allow God to take over and give you the strength to be the best you can be and love your children as precious and priceless gifts.

The idea of family is very significant as we believe that it was established by God Himself right from the beginning of life, according to Genesis Chapter 1.28. *"God blessed them and said to them, Be fruitful and increase in number."* God's initial plan for humanity was that men and women would marry, become one and bear children within a family. Genesis 2:24.

The concept of single parenting is a very contentious subject, a cultural myth, a social dilemma, a religious and a global concern. To the parents who find themselves single inadvertently or as a matter of choice, they have a noble duty and incredible strengths to love, nurture and protect their children by all means. It does not matter whether one is a single father or a single mother, they all face the prevailing challenges equally in my personal view.

Contemporary society has labeled single parenting a taboo and all those families involved as victims of social failure. Their children are victims of stereotypical, conservative, berated individuals who don't understand that they are only children and innocent. The social stigma against a single parent is very strong globally. They are peceived negatively whether in places of worship or at work or in their own communities. They are always associated with poverty and immorality and it is in most cases, if not the majority, women who are the victims. The world blames them for the social ills of society and for producing male villains who fill the prisons. I may say that of course this is not everyone's view. Remember there are many more people who appreciate single parents and see their worth. To all those offenders behind bars: some, if not most of them, feel remorse for what they have done and a few I have spoken to talk well of their mothers who raised them and feel sorry that they have let their mothers, wives and children down.

Why not include some men on the blame stage because they equally contribute to the bearing of these children then run away from their responsibility? This has nothing to do with race, men are men and please do not get me wrong, not all men are irresponsible. Conversely, any woman from any background can also behave irresponsibly. So, I am not defending those who are irresponsible. I am speaking on behalf of every woman who is a single mother and faces the daily challenges of single motherhood. Meanwhile, for those who may be regarded irresponsible, they need support and guidance too. That is how society will get better. It is however, irrational to imagine that the prejudices and bigotry in society can be completely eliminated. Life is life!

My heart also goes out to single fathers. They deserve better. Rather than blame single mothers and how they are parasites of the welfare system, let the governments strictly initiate policies that will focus on working with and supporting every single mother to get them out of poverty. This can be done through encouraging them to start small businesses, by being offered some incentives, reskilling those who need essential employability skills and help find jobs for them after, then pay for the child care which they find difficult to deal with.

Already here in the UK, many single mothers are striving to study and work while taking a huge responsibility for ensuring their children are well and still attend school regularly. Many of them are actually successful, they are employed and fully supporting their children. Some have managed to purchase properties and are able to run their own businesses. Their children are so far doing well in school. So, instead of focusing on those who may still be struggling to make ends meet, or those who are irresponsible, let us try and support them in order to make the world a better place. The fact remains, that we can never have a hundred percent perfect families or perfect children or perfect husbands or perfect wives. If you know of a society free of such imperfections, then it is the first one of its kind on the face of the earth.

In the eyes of the world, an ideal, perfect, traditional, conventional family is the nuclear family of mother, father and children happily living together under one roof. If otherwise, it is a dysfunctional family, not suitable for the upbringing of children. What is important is to embrace these single parent families as part of God's major plan too and be aware that He cares and loves them as much as everybody else. They are unique. They are very special people and their children are equally deserving, beautiful, adorable and innocent. The negative impression and perception towards a single parent is totally unacceptable.

A single parent is a hero who plays the role of two parents in the absence of the other. A single parent is an all rounder who becomes a teacher, a mentor, a supervisor, a physician, a taskmaster, bread winner, driver and watchman over her or his children. Single mothers and single fathers deserve to be applauded rather than being mocked and despised by society. They are a symbol of undiminished love after the loss of a loved partner or painful divorce or having gone through all the disappointments and hustle they endure at the hands of those who let them down and abandon them expecting them to raise their innocent children that they both bring into this world. Single parents have many more strengths, besides gifting humanity, than weaknesses to be blamed for. Only strong parents can build strong families regardless of the prevailing challenges.

Stay with me as we venture together through the spectacular world of the single parenting expedition.

[Google Image]

"You don't choose your family. They are God's gift to you, as you are to them"
Desmond Tutu

"Nothing is more rewarding than to see the look on a happy child's face and know that it's there because of you"
Conover Swofford

"If you want to be in your children's memories tomorrow, you have to be in their lives today."
Anonymous

Simple Ways to Bless Your Day - single parent

- Take joy in the gift of today
- Count your blessings
- Celebrate your successes
- Be thankful for everything especially your children
- Shine in the light of God's love
- Always speak the truth and don't be afraid to say no
- Forgive and forget
- Forgiveness releases you from hurting and it is a key to God's Blessings
- Reach out to other people
- Grow gracefully
- Seek simplicity
- Obey with a cheerful heart
- Stand and be counted
- Be true to your beliefs
- Encourage your children and those around you
- Invest your time in things that matter
- Fuel and keep your faith
- Fill your life with love
- Share the goodness of God

- Be strong in the Lord
- Pursue what is true
- Never compare yourself with anyone, you are unique
- Know exactly what you want in life and pursue it
- Intuition is the teaching from within, listen with your heart
- Develop a strong sense of inner stabilty and security
- Delight in creation
- Memorise the Scriptures
- Celebrate God's promises
- Say your prayers
- Believe in miracles
- Set out to reach your goal
- Live the life
- If you are having a bad day, focus on the positives and your achievements and keep smiling
- Relax, be cheerful and live in the moment

From a Christian Poster

Keep Your Energy High:

Daily Affirmations Of a Single Parent

◆ I am a blessed Mum - I am a blessed Dad◆

◆ Thank you God for my beautiful Children◆

◆ I recognise my value because I am a product of God's love◆

◆ I embrace each day with gratitude and stay focused◆

◆ I build my children's self esteem and self confidence◆

◆ I recognise God as my true source and provider◆

◆ I have unlimited energy and I am enthusiastic to take care of them◆

◆ I am patient with them and I teach them principles of life◆

◆ I put my painful past behind me and embrace my future◆

◆ No matter how hard it seems I will carry on to the end◆

◆ I have all it takes to be a good parent and have a happy disposition◆

◆ I believe my dreams are possible, I walk by faith and not by sight◆

◆ I am entrusted with these children because I am able to take care of them◆

◆ I radiate love, peace, joy and poise. God's best plan involves us◆

◆ I accept myself the way I am and I love myself unconditionally◆

◆ I am willing to learn for my personal growth and improve my life◆

◆ I think healthy thoughts and I pursue what is true◆

◆ I balance my life and I can manage my responbilities everyday◆

◆ I choose to be happy and I appreciate other people in my life◆

◆ I change negative thoughts and worries to positive thoughts◆

◆ Each day that comes is a blessing to me and my children◆

◆ I am strong I am confident I am peaceful I walk in safety◆

◆ I have unlimited support to take care of my children◆

◆ My children are blessed gifted and talented◆

◆My children have a purpose in this world and they will accomplish it◆

◆Thank you God for the wonderful people you bring into my life◆

"Above all, challenge yourself. You may surprise yourself of what strengths you have and what you can accomplish"
Cecil Springer

"When you are but a parent raising a family, you must balance your perspectives between training times and favoring sometimes. It is not easy. But is easier when you are aware of the need to do both. I share these things with you so you can understand some of the differences in our contribution to the children. When you understand them, you will know better how to pray and how to fill the gap. Your children can be successful even with one parent. None of us come from completely ideal situations whether we have two parents or one. Life tends to ensure that all of us gain some exposure to broken areas. Yet God is able to mend the cracks and span the breach that life has left uncovered"

"Yes, you can take a broken home and still produce a straight, intelligent, progressive child. It will require special effort and extra attention to problem areas, but when it's over you will beam with pride and say, I did it myself." Just remember that God was behind the scenes. He helped others overcome disadvantages, and He will help you"

Adapted from "Help! I'm Raising My Children Alone" by T.D. Jakes.

Prayer

T.D.Jakes

Father, it is as we recognise our worth to you that we can begin to walk in the confidence and assurance regardless of what others may say or do. Help us to anchor our lives on your love. Let us call out to you, as did David, "In you, O Lord, I have taken refuge: let me never be put to shame; deliver me in your righteousness. Turn your ear to me, come quickly to my rescue" (Ps. 31:1-2, NIV).

Father, even David, whom you loved so much, felt worthless to the people around him. He called out to you, saying" I am the utter contempt of my neighbours; I am a dread to my friends – those who see me on the streets flee from me . . . For I hear the slander of many" (vv.11-13, NIV). But he knew that you loved him , for he said" But I trust in you, O Lord; I say you are my God" (v.14, NIV).

Help each of my children – and me – to know that you are just waiting to help us when we need you. No matter what happens to us – no matter what others say or think about us – "Praise be to the Lord, for He showed his wonderful love to me when I was in a besieged city" (v.21, NIV).

Thank you Father for making us somebodies in you! Amen.

Adapted from "Help! I'm Raising My Children Alone" by T.D. Jakes pg.117

Chapter One

What is Single Parenting?

Single parenting is an expression refering to an adult who has no spouse, female or male, and with a child or children under the age of 18 in their sole care and having full responsibility to provide primary care for them. This parent fulfills both roles of a mother and father within the family structure.

The majority of single parents globally, are mothers rather than fathers, and although this book will tackle on single fatherhood, It will mainly focus on single motherhood through personal experience. I salute both single mothers and single fathers equally for their relentless strength and motivation. The concept of single parenting is not for the faint-hearted. If at some point you might not agree with some of the sentiments and concepts here within this book, go on to the next page. Views and opinions will vary as a matter of fact.

I am not ashamed to be called a single mother because I have what it takes to be one. It takes audacity, great strength, patience, faith, courage and unconditional love to be a successful, steady, single parent. Not that I do not make mistakes, but rather I accept that mistakes are part of learning and we as parents must accept that we make lots of mistakes along the way as we try to nurture our children. These attributes are of immeasurable value. So far, I have successfully managed with the hand of God upon me for the past fifteen good years and now coming to sixteen. As I stand at the moment, it is this distinctivess of single motherhood and the attributes I possess as an individual that defines who I am.

The fact remains that life is very challenging. I have spent half my life crying to God over so many sensitive issues in my personal life but very grateful for the courage and energy that no matter what, I keep going. Many times my son has seen me cry and hugged me telling that "mum, things will be alright for us", but I cry more when I am on my own and I find comfort in that. I am not as outgoing as I used to be simply because I would not want to leave my son on his own. I just want to be there for him and I know when he is grown and independent, I will have time to myself but at the moment I will give him my time and all the attention and love he needs.

When he was little, every time he saw me crying he would also cry with me then I would stop knowing it will have a negative effect on his well being as a child and as a boy. As he is grown into a teen now, amazingly, he has got so much wisdom and fortitude that he reads me scriptures and motivating and inspiring words teaching me to be confident and positive. He constantly reminds me that mum *"Mind over matter, be positive"*. He says he has nothing to worry about because after all things will get better for us. He is such a gem. He has answers to everything and I just feel very safe and secure with him. Most friends call him my bodyguard because we are ever together.

The Bible says God puts our tears in his bottle in Psalm 56: 8. You cry and let out the heaviness and life goes on. I decided I was not going to re marry or date again even when I thought it was essential for both of us. To me, getting involved in another relationship meant if the man is not right or does not love my son, then I would not be a good mother. I was determined and have always been, to be there for him constantly and give him the love I never had as a child, give him everything he wants as long as I can afford, teach him to be a self disciplined child who can be a role model to others.

Of course, there are times I wish I could have someone in our lives for companionship. It is very necessary for a man to be in a family as there are certain things that men can do very well than women especially DIY and of course for security. I still pray that when time is right, God will bring along my way the rightful person. I of course appreciate the role that men play in a family and the joy they can bring.

My wish is that he grows up to be a great husband and father who will be there for his wife and children. One spiritual mentor that God brought along in my life at one of the most challenging moments of my life as a single, helpless mother was when he and his wife gave me a book called *"Yesterday I Cried"* by Iyanla Vazant. I met this couple in a church I was introduced to by my dear friend and from that time I learnt to view life from a different perspective.

I don't know where I would be without my dear son in my life. His presence throughout both our lives has shaped me into a disciplined and focused individual, not that I am not or that I haven't always been, but I am a role model to him, ensuring I do the right things and conduct myself in the manner that can directlty or indirectly shape and guide him to follow suit and learn from me. I have since grown a great deal and made substantial strides in my life, careful for every decision I make, and every step I take, well aware that whatever I do, will have either a negative or positive impact on my son's life. This is a decision-making process that makes you realise that having children in your life makes life so delicate and different. You are no longer your own completely but your children share a huge part of your life. Each day you realise that as they grow, routines shift, responsibilities change, needs increase, parent-child relationships either grow stronger or diminish with time.

In my case, nevertheless, our parent-child love and relationship keeps growing stronger and we are such great friends, there are certain things however, that you will need to approve or accept or disapprove as a parent, such as habits they pick up from their friends, but what you instill in him initially is what cements the roots of his entire being as an individual.

I can proudly say that I was once happily married and although this joy did not last due to unavoidable circumstances, the outcome of that marriage is my beautiful child, my son, as the evidence. I have many wonderful memories of great times I enjoyed as a wife, and I appreciate my husband regardless of his flaws. He will forever remain the father of my son and be remembered for all the good attributes he possessed that have been passed on to our son. He was not perfect and neither am I, because no one on this planet earth is perfect. Anything tragic that happened to disintegrate our family life was beyond our control. When certain things happen in our lives that we have no control over, we can still count on God's love and strength to carry us through as we heal and look to full restoration. Life goes on regardless of circumstances.

Many individuals from broken families look back and think maybe that had they dealt differently with the challenges they both encountered, they could have made their marriages work and they could have lasted a lifetime together. We all desire to enjoy our marital relationships and wish we could, as couples and partners, withstand any challenges and grow old together to be able to watch our children grow old enough to fly the nest and become independent. The fact remains that no one ever knows what is likely to happen anytime. We all take each day as it comes hoping and expecting the best as long as it takes.

Sometimes, when things tend not to work out as we expected from the beginning, we start focusing on the other person's flaws instead of our own, and in the end it turns into a blame game rather than endure to find solutions so we can sustain the marriage and support each other. More often than not, of course, couples first try to sustain their marriages, but it is when they feel nothing and no one can heal the broken hearts that consequently they decide to let go. Either one of the two decides eventually, to walk out without analysing the future consequences of making hasty decisions on life's matters like marriage that involve the innocent children or the two of you may agree on a concrete solution. However, at times it can, looking back, be healthy and balanced for the remaining parent and children, if all attempts to heal the problems have failed. Single parenting will always reflect a negative impression upon anybody but that is part of life.

It does not matter whether you were once married or not, but you have children, that's what counts most. Be proud of that. You are a parent. Celebrate it and count each moment as valuable. That's what makes you special. I love Oprah Winfrey. She is one of my best role models, bless her. She has brought the world together, helped reconciled broken families, healed broken hearts and touched the lives of millions of children around the world, yet she has none of her own. She is a hero and a mother in the lives of those young girls in South Africa where she decided to give an opportunity to girls from underprivileged families to have education. Yet she was brought up in a broken family herself and has had her own challenges growing up. I can identify with her upbringing.

My other role model and a woman who has endured the worst hardships I know of, yet made it to where she is, is Iyanla Vazant. I can identify with her rough upbringing, first with her grandmother, then her single mother whose husband played very little in the upbringing of their children's lives. Later, herself as single mother, life was almost unbearable. Reading her breathtaking books; *Yesterday I Cried"* and *"Peace from Broken Pieces"* sends a chill up your spine. You get to certain pages and you tell yourself, "ok I can't carry on" as you can't imagine what is coming next whether she will survive or not. Now, she helps mend broken lives and reconciles families and broken relationships through her series; *"Iyanla: Fix My Life"* on OWN (Oprah Winfrey Network). Life is a journey and whether a single parent or not, young or an adult, the grace of God is ever sufficient to carry us through no matter how painful or difficult the journey may be, as long as we don't give up.

Joyce Meyer is another woman of substance that I greatly admire. She is not a single parent but she has endured so much pain from childhood to where she is now. She is now a renowned world preacher who prays and encourages other women to trust God. Her books especially *"Beauty For Ashes"* is a worth read, and *"The Battlefield of The Mind"*. There are several books she has written that will inspire you in your journey.

T.D Jakes inspiring book of *"Help! I am Raising My Children Alone"* is a must read for every single parent. Also *"Woman Thou Art Loosed"*

If you are single or married with no children, you are still special in the eyes of God and those around you who love you for who you are. God loves us for who we are and not what other people think of us. That's what matters. Know that God has pledged a great value on you regardless of what you have or what you do not have at the moment. Place the same value on yourself and start seeing life from a positive perspective. Things change as time goes by, life gets better. There is no permanent situation.

My experience of single motherhood has been that it is a worthwhile journey. It is not an easy one especially when you have to meet every single need for yourself and your child or children with limited resources. However, what is important is to embrace the journey and enjoy every moment with your children regardless of prevailing challenges. When you focus on the beauty and innocence of your children, all other worries tend to fade away.

There is no utopian world or flawless person, but we all have the grace of God equally and we are all capable of accomplishing anything we desire to. On this note therefore, it is up to each one of us as individuals to choose to believe and walk with God knowing that with Him in us, and with us, we can overcome and deal with every challenge, or we can decide to walk it all alone and strain to manage everything in our own strength. This however, means we feel separate from God who gives us the strength and guidance we constantly need day by day, day in and day out.

God will still love us for who we are regardless of whether we acknowledge him or not. However, He is much happier when you choose to entrust your entire life upon Him and surrender to Him, casting all your burdens to Him so He can be on the steering wheel of your life's journey. You don't have to be perfect to earn God's love, grace, promises and his other divine benefits, because there isn't any one perfect on this entire globe. Not even the heroes of the Bible or all other prophets of other religions we read about and try to emulate were without fault.

In fact it was because when God called them as in the Christian Bible to delegate them as his ambassadors, he exactly knew they had their imperfections as human beings, but chose to focus on their strengths of willingness and obedience to his calling and mission. Some of them were leading messed-up lives and some of them had a background of a broken past.

The Bible makes a reference to the first single mother in the Bible in Genesis 21; Hagar and her son Ishmael. Regardless of how the boy was born, God still loved and cared and provided for him and her mother. She must have been mocked by her community as a shameful woman but God still chose to bless them.

Other single parent references in the Bible include:

God is *"a father of the fatherless"* Psalm 68:5

Proverbs 15:25 *The LORD will destroy the house of the proud: but He will establish the border of the widow.*

Isaiah 54:4 *Fear not; for thou shalt not be ashamed: neither be thou confounded; for thou shalt not be put to shame: for thou shalt forget the shame of thy youth, and shalt not remember the reproach of thy widowhood any more.*

Jeremiah 49:11 *Leave thy fatherless children, I will preserve [them] alive; and let thy widows trust in me.*

Zechariah 7:10 *And oppress not the widow, nor the fatherless, the stranger, nor the poor; and let none of you imagine evil against his brother in your heart.*

Luke 18:3 *And there was a widow in that city; and she came unto him, saying, Avenge me of mine adversary.*

Chapter 18:5 states that *"Yet because this widow troubleth me, I will avenge her, lest by her continual coming she weary me."*

James 1:27 *"Pure religion and undefiled before God and the Father is this, To visit the fatherless and widows in their affliction, [and] to keep himself unspotted from the world."*

My favourite author and true man of God, the late Derek Prince, whose legacy has been preserved by UCB Radio of Bob Gas, so that you can think the man is still alive, teaches a great deal on single parents and fatherless children. His little book that I have had since 2004, and I still read it again and again, puts emphasis on how the fatherless and widows should be treated:

"Who cares for Orphans, Widows, the Poor and Oppressed, God does... Do We?

I can guarantee you that life becomes a fascinating experience and worthwhile living, when you choose to trust and walk by faith at any cost, like a child fully convinced that your God loves and cares for you. A child gets shouted at but then cries and runs toward the very parent who has made him cry because he or she can only see this mum or dad as the only saviour to run to. Have you ever tried throwing a little child in the air and kept your eyes on him or her with your arms open to catch them? What do they do? Do they scream in fear? No, they smile and laugh in excitement assured that you will definitely catch them back. I am sure their heart would be pumping but they know they are safe. That's the simplest approach we need to take and be strong enough knowing that no matter how difficult it is for us in life, or no matter how far we have been tossed up, our dear God is ever watching with his loving, open hands ready to catch us back safely so that we are not hurt or completely damaged in the process of adversity and pain.

Not that life will not be without any challenges, but you can rest assured that in your darkest and lowest moments, God is ever available to hold your trembling hand and calm your throbbing heart, walking you through the painful path, pulling you away and healing you from shame and guilt, condemnation and accusations, hopelessness and misery, dispair and anxiety, anger and bitterness and all feelings of doubts and disappointments that you may encounter, or knowing that He goes an extra mile willingly to carry you on His shoulders bearing all your fears and pains, guiding you in the right direction.

Each individual human being can testify that at our worst and lowest moments in life, there is always a voice, a soft loving spirit within us that reassures us when we are at our worst, when we let it whisper to us and says *"its alright" "you can do it" "keep going"* and so on and so forth. The sweet, small voice within each one of us is a guarantee that that it is not over yet.

"Let yourself enjoy being you today. Allow the anger, the anxiety, the frustration and the stress to fall away. Stop assuming that you must be negative just because of your circumstances. Wherever you are, whatever you're doing, just let yourself enjoy. Let yourself enjoy being alive and involved in this day. There are challenges, there is beauty, there is pain, there is joy. Immerse yourself in it all and enjoy the intensity of your living experience. The harsh words directed your way keep you focused. The kindnesses build your faith. The disappointments give you wisdom and perspective. The triumphs make

it all worthwhile. In every moment there is every possibility. Could anything be more sublime? Live those moments with an unassailable sense of enjoyment. They're yours to live, to experience, to mould and to elevate. Don't fall down into the world. Bring it up to you, and enjoy".

From My Way Daily Motivator. September 5, 2010

Many single parents will perhaps live in constant shame, guilt and self-condemnation as if the reason they are single was because they were not good enough and that's why their partners abandoned them, or that they made big mistakes to have these children out of wedlock without their fathers or mothers around, or that they are simply failures at family building. They then succumb to what society has labelled them - as failures and outcasts. Its my greatest prayer that this social stigma must change especially at such a time as this with idea of changing social values. Individual people choose the way they want to live and do as they wish such as altering their sexuality or marry whomsoever they want. Life styles vary depending on choices. However, the single parent lives on the edge of society because she seemingly has no rightful place in an ideal family world. She and her children are viewed as an abberration to society, yet she may have have made a healthy choice to live on her own with her children to avoid all kinds of problems involved with having a wrong partner or an irresponsible father. In case of those parents with children who decide to devorce, most often they realise that it could be the best option to bring up children in a more peaceful and independent environment than where there is too much confrontation and fighting.

You don't have to live this way anymore. Just believe and change your perspective of life, that in essence, life is full of possibilities and opportunities to live happily, whether you are a single parent, single person or happily married. Your capacity for joy and healthy living is not dependent on any particular situation, activity or outcome, but what you as individual make sense of the infinite power you possess within you to transform your life. When we think we are alone and cannot carry on, there is always a loving, supportive, invisible hand behind us.

Have you ever read the *"Poem of God's Footprints"*?

Footprints in the Sand

One night a man had a dream. He dreamed He was walking along the beach with the LORD. Across the sky flashed scenes from His life. For each scene He noticed two sets of footprints in the sand. One belonging to Him and the other to the LORD.

When the last scene of His life flashed before Him, he looked back at the footprints in the sand. He noticed that many times along the path of His life there was only one set of footprints. He also noticed that it happened at the very lowest and saddest times of His life.

This really bothered Him and He questioned the LORD about it. LORD you said that once I decided to follow you, you'd walk with me all the way. But I have noticed that during the most troublesome times in my life there is only one set of footprints. I don't understand why when I needed you most you would leave me.

The LORD replied, my precious, precious child, I Love you and I would never leave you! During your times of trial and suffering when you see only one set of footprints, it was then that I carried you.

[Google image]

"God is not man that he should lie, nor a son of man, that he should change his mind. Does he speak and then not act? Does he promise and not fulfill?"

"For I know the plans I have for you, declares the Lord. Plans to prosper you and not to harm you, plans to give you hope and a *future. Then you will call upon me and come and pray to me, and I will listen to you".* Jeremiah 29: 11-12. What a promise!

In the earlier chapters of the book of Jeremiah chapter 14: 7-8, it is written that *"Blessed is the man that trusts in the Lord, and whose hope the Lord is. He shall be as a tree planted by the waters, and that spreads out her green roots by the river, and shall not be seen when the heat comes but her leaf shall be green; and shall not be careful in the year of drought, neither shall cease from yealding fruit".*

When you humble yourself and place all your confidence in God, he will energise you, heal you, beautify you, dignify you, satisfy you, strengthen you and constantly renew your strength as with eagles and make you stay youthful, aging beautifully like fine wine so you can keep your visions alive before you, enjoying bringing up your lovely children. You will bear fruit and become a fountain benefiting others around you. You will have a positive outlook and be able able to build healthy friendships. Simply ask God through prayer to restore everthing that has been taken away from you. He will restore and rebuild the broken walls of your crumbling world.

Choose your associations and acquaintances carefully, for in most cases, wrong friends can hinder us from advancing into what we want to become. Sometimes our desires and dreams may differ from those of close acquaintances, and they will want you to stay together in the same situations especially if they are despondent and do not really expect much in life anymore. Whenever you want to move on and give meaning to your life, they may discourage you. So the best way is to transform your own life first and be their role model so they learn from you.

God created you for a special purpose on this earth and He will ensure you live to accomplish that purpose. As the author of *"Purpose Driven Life"* Rick Warren of Saddleback Church in California, reminds us that we were made by God and for God, and that until we understand that concept, life will not make sense. He goes on to say that the moment you learn your purpose in life, it will make you endeavour to focus on what is important and what matters in life, hence becoming *"effective and selective"*.

How wonderful and empowering to know that once you are aware of your purpose in life, it *"motivates you and prepares you for eternity"*. When he teaches on the significance of each of us becoming best friends of God, Rick further highlights the fact that *"Knowing and loving God is our great privilege, and being known and loved by God is God's greatest pleasure"*. How beautiful to know that our lives are not in vain. The ultimate truth is that God's major plan for us is to live healthy, live long, be happy and prosper.

I am not of the ideology that God does not want us to prosper, I am not of the view of most religious fanatics who preach against prosperity and persuade innocent people that being poor is God's plan for mankind. Poverty has led to many broken marriages and it creates misery in society. It is poverty that leads to many people getting involved in all sorts of crime because they want to transform their lives. It is poverty that leads individuals to choose to become false preachers and prophets so they can solicit large sums of money from their congregation for their own good. It is poverty that drives young people and adults equally into substance abuse to escape depression. It is poverty that leads young, vulnerable beautiful women into prostitution so they can earn some income.

Our loving God wants us healthy and happy and prosperous. Whether single parents or married couples, when they are financially independent and living by God's principles, they are happy and a blessing to society. Society will condemn single parents or unmarried people or divorced preachers and will not look to them as role models, but in my opinion, they all fufill God's purpose equally.

Appreciate the fact that you are not alone. You have a God you can rely on by faith to carry you and your children through the most trying moments. Some of you may have great support from close family and friends and others from your church community or faith groups. I strongly believe that having a lovely, innocent child or children in your care at no fault of your own, God ensures that He provides and protects all of you at all costs. You will meet very kind and loving people along the way who will not judge you, but accept you and love you as you are.

Some people however, will treat you differently with contempt because you seem a failure and lonely in their eyes and before the world. You may be blamed for what you are going through, but you must stay focused and seek good in every situation. Albert Einstein states that *"In the midst of difficulty, lies opportunity"*. Focus on what you want to accomplish and let your children be the reason you are alive today. The challenges you face today will become the joys of tomorrow if you don't give them permission to disable and obscure your vision. You know what you want and what you are going through now may simply be a transitional process to a better and bright future for you and your children. You must persevere, be strong for yourself and for them. If you break, they will break too. You are their pillar and tower for their support.

You will notice that you might not fit well in certain situations or company of certain people, but remember you are not alone. God accepts you as you are. I have first hand experience where I have felt or been made to feel that I am out of place whenever I am in the company of married couples. You do not feel free because as a single woman, your very good married friends will consciouly or subconciously feel insecure around you and their husbands. They will suspect you of being a target or even interested in their husbands which can be a very unfortunate and shameful perception from some close friends. For reasons like this, I rarely interact with certain groups of people and this is where I seem like a lonely person. Even if some others may not suspect you, it is so obvious that in a gathering where many people are couples, you as a single person will not fit. As a matter of fact, I have always found comfort and peace in the company of my own son, just having him around me gives me such pride that at least I am a mother and nothing else matters.

There are millions of single parents out there who are happily taking care of their children and positively contributing to their communities and to the world at large. I am sure not many people would wish to be single parents unless you have been there and have had a bad experience with your partner. The truth is; two heads are better than one in every way as long as they can be there for each other. To some, it may be a choice because they want their total independence. This is absolutely desirable as well.

A happy and healthy family is essential and ideal for the upbringing of children. As a matter of fact, many successful families have produced healthy and successful children who later in life become responsible adults themselves. To others they have had their challenges too. There are successful familes with both parents who have perfectly brought up their children, but still, some of these children choose their own paths and stumble along the way in so many ways to the extent that some will become truants, rebellious teenagers, eventually they become very unsuccessful individuals in life. Their parents will have given them everything but what what they choose to do in life becomes their business.

However, successful families, whether single parent or couple families, all can create a harmonious and thriving community and become part of a progressive nation. They can all have family values and they are able to sustain generations of more healthy, happy families. Although a family with both parents was God's original plan, single parent families are also in God's promised plan. Every one is included in God's plan because his spirit is in everyone of us.

But does it mean that single parent families should be viewed as dysfunctional families? Not at all. There is evidence of many successful single parent families that have produced some of the finest people we know in our contemporary society and in the times past. They themselves are a blessing to the world. You will read about some individual examples in this book in later chapters.

Analysing the causes of single parenting, you will discover that there is no guarantee that a happy family will stay happy for ever. Anything can happen such as sudden death through accidents, illnesses through natural causes, wars through political instability that automatically disperse families or even as a result of a couple's own failures to keep the promises. These factors don't necessarily turn them into dysfunctional families. Although there will be a gap in that family after one parent is gone, it is still possible for one strong surviving parent to manage and keep the family running while maintaining its integrity.

It is amazing how single parenting has been demonised. Children from these families become victims of social stigma and prejudice. You will be shocked at how society has this belief system that most crimes are committed by children brought up by single mothers. To some extent yes, but even some of the crimes are committed by those from well-to-do families. It is not conclusive. All human beings are capable of falling short and making mistakes in life. If you are a hundred percent flawless, I salute you.

As a single parent of a teenage son, I have set my own family values and principles. I have to remain a role model in his life and set examples he can follow. My one desire is to see him grow into a disciplined, respectful and responsible adult. As a black boy in a society where black boys have become victims of prejudice and labelled as street gangs and under achievers, every parent from ethnic minority background still wants the best for their children. Although not everyone will view all black boys like that, but the social stigma still lingers quite strongly. The truth is, all parents, single or couples want the best for their children regardless of background, race or belief system.

I sit down with him in a relaxed environment and we discuss issues that affect both of us. We discuss his learning needs, we discuss his personal interests and any emotional issues. We discuss my parenting skills and I have to listen to his opinions and views. I try as much to monitor his activities and I know most of his friends. They are good boys from all kinds of family backgrounds and ethnic groups that I don't have to worry about them influencing him badly in any way. They have known one another from their old primary school to his current secondary school. Others are from our local church where he is part of the youth team. I encourage him not to be a bad influence on them either.

We spend quality time together, we chat, we joke, we laugh, we watch his TV programs together. Even If I don't have to, I know what he seems to like. We treat ourselves whenever we can and we enjoy each other's company at a mother son level. I teach him the fear of God above everything else. I teach him to have self control and respect for others. Remember that every parent will still do the best for their children, but when they grow up they find their way in life, they may fail and fall as human beings, but the blame must not be imposed on parents. If children are out of hand when they are still little, yes, but once they have grown up as adults, then they must be responsible for their own actions.

Creflo Dollar states that children must be taught self control because it can be difficult to impart anything in a child who is out of control. Taffi Dollar writes that *"Train up a child without breaking his spirit."* She refers to the instructions and insights provided in the Bible concerning good parenting. Proverbs 22:6 teaches that *"Train up a child in the way he should go: and when he is old, he will not depart from it."* There is a saying that goes thus; *"Bend a stick when it is still tender, once it is dry, when you try bending it, it will break."* In other words, it is important to try and shape your children when they are still tender and shapeable. At least if they divert away from your advice as adults, they will remember that you did your best to show them the right path. They will have no excuse to blame you, but be responsible for their own actions.

Again the Bible teaches in Colossians 3:20-21 that *"Children obey your parents in everything, for this is pleasing to the Lord. Fathers do not provoke or irritate or fret your children lest they become dicouraged and sullen and morose and frustrated."*

The way you talk to your children is the way they will respond. If you discipline them in anger and frustration, they will resent you. If you have been disappointed by a child's father or mother, do not seek revenge through the child. Do not punish them for their father's or their mother's misdeeds, they are only innocent. Teach them the opposite instead.

Always tell your child or children that you love them; Say "I love you" as he goes to bed and before he leaves for school and every time you speak to him on the phone and so on and so forth. It is a kind of reassurance that you sincerely mean what you say.

My favourite piece of Poem on how children learn through what they they experience.

CHILDREN LEARN WHAT THEY LIVE
Dorothy Law Nolte

If a child lives with criticism, he learns to condemn.
If a child lives with hostility, he learns to fight.
If a child lives with fear, he learns to be apprehensive.
If a child lives with pity, he learns to feel sorry for himself.
If a child lives with ridicule, he learns to be shy.
If a child lives with jealousy, he learns what envy is.
If a child lives with shame, he learns to feel guilty.
If a child lives with encouragement, he learns to be confident.
If a child lives with tolerance, he learns to be patient.
If a child lives with praise, he learns to be appreciative.

If a child lives with acceptance, he learns to love.
If a child lives with approval, he learns to like himself.
If a child lives with recognition, he learns that it is good to have a goal.
If a child lives with sharing, he learns about generosity.
If a child lives with honesty and fairness, he learns what truth and justice are.
If a child lives with security, he learns to have faith in himself and in those about him.
If a child lives with friendliness, he learns that the world is a nice place in which to live.
If you live with serenity, your child will live with peace of mind.
With what is your child living?

"Children are apt to live up to what you believe in them."
Lady Bird Johnson

Dr. James Dobson in his famous book *"Bringing up Boys"* pg. 229. clearly states that *"Self discipline is a worthwhile goal, but it rarely develops on its own initiative. It must be taught. Shaping and moulding young minds is a product of careful and dilligent parental leadership. You can be sure it requires great effort and patience."*

This is a powerful lesson for all of us, single parents or married couples or anyone else with children of any age in their care. Parenting is both a natural gift and a learned skill. As a parent, learn as much as you can for the sake of gaining the right skills to bring up your children in the right way. Take the responsibility to train your own child and be their role model. You are their first contact, teach them your family and moral values. Being a single parent does not hinder you to do this. It is never easy, but it is possible. You are their teacher for life. The moment a child comes into a person's life, roles and responsibilities automatically shift to suit the needs and requirements of the new arrival in the family. Children will then naturally grow and develop healthily, knowing that they are are well cared and loved and given more than just the provision of the basic needs.

You will agree with me that when children are contented and disciplined from home, and very respectful of their own parents, they will always respect teachers equally because they see teachers as their role models too. When a child has behavioural issues in school, the best way to support them and deal with the problem is to identify if there are any family issues interfering with his personal life. Once this is established, it is easier to be able to provide support for both child and parent. All parents are born teachers to shape the young minds, to shape the future and help shape the world of tomorrow.

In my case there are, however, boundaries when I need to get tough on my son to remind him of his responsibilities such as sharing the house chores and him cleaning his room or ironing his school uniform. Believe me, it's not always that smooth, straightforward thing, but he does it anyway. At least he is responsive and he never complains. In most cases when children learn their responsibilities well in advance, they will enjoy fulfilling them without reminders and when they do this, they deserve a lot of praise. I will still remember to reward him or simply say thank you for washing up or sorting out your room. That's when he smiles. I notice that as he gets older, he just does things without a reminder which, as a parent I find impressive. For instance, we have been discussing about the grass needing cutting, I came from work and found that he had already done it on his own initiative. He then left me a note that he had gone to skate in the park with his friends as it is a holiday. I sent him a text to thank him and told him that he can buy himself a big Mac. He naturally loves that. Praise is magic for every child.

Praise and rewards towards children for good behaviour or accomplished chores or any achievement at school as we know it, increases a child's self esteem and they will want to have more and more praise, so they can feel appreciated. Consequently, they will add more effort next time or they will do it wilingly on their own initiative so as to surprise you and earn a quick thank you. I notice that Supper Nanny on the TV program uses that techinique quite often for impossible kids when helping some families deal with their children and it works wonders. You will notice that it is not necessarily single parent families with difficult children, it is all families. Isn't it like getting good feedback from your teacher at school with that smiley stamp written *"Excellent"* or *"Well done"* or *"You are A Star."*

Even as adult students at college or university, when you get good feedback from your lecturer on your assignments, you will feel good. As an employee, when you are rewarded for your efficiency, commitment or outstanding, hard work, you add more effort because you feel elated. We all need medals when we do well. This response is a natural instinct and an incentive for all of us to excel in everything we do.

As much as most or all children love gifts, they prefer their parents' attention and affection. They love to be hugged and want to hear you tell them that you love them so much. Look them straight in the eyes with approval and a smile. Actively listen to what they always have to say. They love to be told that that they are beautiful and smart. Go shopping together. They have their own choices of brands and trendy fashions as they grow. Always allow them their preferences.

Children want to be praised for their effort at school and every progress and achievement they make. Constantly maintain that positive reinforcement to keep them motivated. If they don't do well, don't scold them, simply encourage them and let them know that they still have the potential to do better. Check and monitor their school work. Read through their teachers' comments or feedback together. Sign their planners on time and give comments where required. Constantly work through with them where they might need help or some guidance.

Make it a duty to see that they are in a tidy environment at home, their room is clean and condusive for learning. Check that they have those essential things they need for home work like pencils, pens, rulers, rubbers, extra texts if possible, internet is now affordable. They need a good bag to carry all their "stuff" they need including the PE kit and a snack. Ensure they always have breakfast in the morning. This is a key to their learning as it gives them energy to stay alert and contributes to their performance, especially if it is with a good type of cereal. It is your responsibility as a parent to make sure a child sleeps on time and wakes up on time for school. Have a clean, pressed uniform for each day, personal hygiene is important. Most children up to the teenage stage do not fancy bathing, whether girls or boys. This can be a big issue but find a way to deal with it. Never let your child go to school unkempt as if they are neglected. If they are ruffled, they will have no friends and can attract bullies. They will have no self esteem or confidence in themselves. I always remind my son that he must be both clean on the outside and in the inside. It is obvious that your outlook will or is likely to portray your private life, I mean in terms of personal hygiene.

It is your duty as a parent to ensure they get to school on time and do not unnecessarily miss classes. If they have after-school activities and clubs, support them. If you are part of every aspect of their lives, it demonstrates your love and total parental responsibility. All these factors positively contribute and enhance not only their academic success but mould them into responsible, self disciplined young people who will not give trouble to their teachers at school or become a problem in their own communities because they have no time for that anyway. Ensure they do not hang along the way after school, that's where they start getting involved in some sneaky behaviour. Yes, they can take their time a little bit to get home while they chat with friends, but be strict on that. A lot of kids hang around certain areas after school especially teens and I watch them misbehave in public. If your child is late a few minutes to arrive home, call them to find out where they are. Groups can be a catalyst of influence for bad behaviour. That is how it all starts, peer pressure is unavoidable, but can be avoided. Talk to your children from the beginning and they will understand. It will make life easier for all of you so you do not have to worry.

Always compile their school work right from the start and reports and certificates of achievements in beautiful folders. It can be fun after a while when you pull out the folder for grade 3 when the children are already in high school and show them how hard they have worked. They look back at how far they have come from and how much they have developed. Looking at the funny pictures they used to draw for you or for themselves is fun. It is the same as pulling out all the family albums when you are relaxed and browsing through the family history reflecting on how much they have grown. These are cherished moments that bring so much joy and good memories and keep you together.

Run and play together while in the park on sunny days. Have a go at their video games. Play some riddles and brain teasers together if you know of any. There are loads on the internet. If you love cycling, join in on a summer's day. If you don't know how to cycle, make an effort to learn. It's a skill for life and healthy for you too. Take long walks or jog together. Dare to go on terrifying rides together. I have had my share on some of them, and I thought I would never do it again, but after surviving one, you line up for the next one again. Watch family movies, prepare meals together, play pranks on each other or even Hide and Seek. If they are little, always let them win, if they lose the game, you are out! As they become teenagers, their interests of course change and they prefer to hang around their close friends, but this does not interfere with your relationship. If you sense it is, keep their movements and behaviour in check. Be tactful to maintain your relationship with them. Just know who their friends are.

Attend their school functions and parents' evenings. Get to know their teachers and enquire how they are getting on at school. Make sure they do not go late or miss school unnecessarily with no good reason. Respond to school correspondences and read their school reports with them, praising them. Ensure they are smart and neat and they have breakfast in the mornings. Teach them the significance of personal hygiene and to love themselves. Girls can be keen on this naturally, including cleaning their own space but it does not come straightforward with some boys in my opinion, they couldn't care less! I mean like throwing socks anywhere around their rooms, under their bed or on top of cupboards. If you are looking for dirty clothes that need washing, they may not necessarily be in the washing basket. Simply look everywhere! Even with some adult men believe me. (*I have no clue why - joke!*). However, my son tries to be neat and "*swag.*" So I salute him for that which I believe he took after his father.

When it comes to his homework, many times I am reminded that I don't know this and that especially if it is a subject I am not familiar with such as Chemistry, Physics or the mighty Mathematics. He says "Mum, I know what to do, trust me." Some times when I get angry at him for some reason, he lets me talk until I finish, then ask if he can explain himself. He says I need to listen to his side before I draw conclusions and get mad at him. It makes sense as a parent when you realise you were wrong. Teach them to let you know if they are going to be late from school so that you don't panic. Do the same whenever you are likely to be running late or to pick them. It is a simple courtesey.

Sometimes as parents we just think we are always right. However, we must realise that we can be wrong at times. Listening to children's views and opinions makes them feel involved, trusted and responsible especially when they are teens. Have you ever noticed naughty, disturbed youngsters when they throw tantrums at school or college? This is from my experience as a teacher and having worked with teens and mentoring them. Their response is always "*Who cares*" or "*I can't be bothered*" or "*I can't be asked.*" Do you ever wonder why? It is not just a rude gesture. It is an outcry for having lack of attention from their parents they love so much. Children who know their parents love them and have a good relationship with them, will always respect teachers and other adults equally. "*Charity begins at home.*" This a common phrase used by both Christians and Muslims to teach about love and responsibilities in the home.

If children are loved and provided for at home, it will reflect in their behaviour outside. Parents should therefore do their best to love and provide for their families first, before they take their courtesies elswhere. It is common that some parents, especially fathers tend to pay more attention to other people's children than their own. Some fathers can give favours to other people than their own families. It is not selfish to provide for your own family first, because they are essentially your primary responsibility. I have a lot of examples from people I have spoken to, both young adults and adults who have expressed their disappointments at their fathers who constantly ignored them as children and declined to provide their essential needs, but decided to support children from other families at the time. These children will feel resentment towards such a parent.

Also teach your children the value of prayer as a family and self reflection. Pray together and give them the opportunity to lead and share their views on faith matters no matter what your belief values are. Some teenagers might not like prolonged prayers, so bear in mind not to strain or bore them too much. A short prayer of thanksgiving is also effective. You don't have to be religious or spiritual to give thanks for the gift of life. It is a natural instinct. Some people will simply say they are grateful for the divine provider, altogether that is acknowledging the existence of God.

Have time to discuss with your children their future ambitions and dreams. Teach them the power of visualisation and positive affirmations to build their confidence and thought process. This naturally raises our energy and enthusiasm as human beings. If you believe in the power of positive thinking, allow them to create their own vision boards. Jesus himself went around teaching the power of faith. You will realise that most of the healings he conducted were successfully based on the faith of those whose lives he changed. All he did was prompt them to reactivate their faith and in the end he would say; *"Your faith has healed you."* This is important in life if we are to attain our goals.

We all need to seek guidance, happiness, peace, love, harmony and security. We must step out and have the willingness to listen and learn from those who already know. Certain things do not just find us, it is our purpose in life to desire to achieve and be happy. Our main desire in life is to be successful. If children are taught these simple essential elements of success from the start, they will be able to sustain them in life. *"Persistence overcomes resistance".* We cannot give up on our children. Even as a single parent of eight children or ten or twelve, you can manage and win.

Encourage your children to read about their role models and about people who changed the world. I love libraries, they are very powerful source of enriching children's learning experience at all levels and fostering literacy development. Encourage them to find books they enjoy based on what they like most. When they are very young, they will enjoy it most having to go in with their parents and spend some good time out there in the library or just borrow as many books for a few weeks. Sign up and become a member of your local library.

Chapter Two

Causes of Single Parenting?

Can anybody determine who is likely to become a single parent or not? If so, how and when? It is an unpredictable phase in life that just happens. Anybody can be at risk of single parenthood whether due to social-economic times where everything keeps changing or, as mentioned above, for unforeseeable reasons. For instance, the wife of Martin Luther King became a single mother due to her husband trying to bring justice to the oppressed and ended up loosing his life, leaving a beautiful wife and children on their own. Many families have lost loved parents due to accidents or illnesses. Many more young families in the UK and America are losing their fathers and husbands in the army leaving their wives and beautiful children on their own. Can society blame them for being single parent families if these mothers never remarry? That would be very harsh and insensitive. A number of factors however, may be causative but they are not exhaustive as detailed in the following sections.

> **Divorce**

Divorce is a legal termination of marital union between two people. It has played a big role in destroying stable families for centuries. There are many factors that contribute to divorce. Whether a couple have been married for one month or two years or ten years or thirty years, nothing seems magic. Anything can happen, and nothing should ever be taken for granted. Divorce affects everyone regardless of age, race, social status, financial security or faith background.

Some of the main causes of divorce can be;

Infidelity, where one spouse becomes unfaithful to the other and starts having extra marital affairs. It could be either the wife or husband. Once proven beyond doubt, the other part can file for divorce according to the law. One of them becomes custodian of the children or they can decide on how to share responsibilities.

Financial pressure can cause couples to fall apart. For instance if one partner is a bread winner and the other one for some reason is not contributing equally, it may cause some misunderstandings and they end up splitting over disagreements. When finances are not enough to cater for family needs, pressure, stress and frustration cause tension. Too many debts bring a heavy burden on the family. It is not healthy for one partner to be totally dependent on the other for everything. Family roles and responsibilities need to be shared equally.

Communication breakdown. With marriages, trust is paramount, respect for each other's point of view, listening to what the other has to say is crucial, transparency, feedback, tolerance, a non-judgmental approach and consequently, understanding each other's needs. If these elements are lacking in a marriage, it is easy for differences to occur and end up in divorce.

Distance marriage. This can be due to one partner having to work away from the family home and spending days, weekends or months away. It's like the missing presence of the other parent results in less attention and eventually the gap closes in. Either of the partner might decide to find temporary company elsewhere and slowly but surely the cracks keep widening. It takes a strong character to maintain a distance relationship.

Broken promises. Newly wed couples will have promised each other heaven and earth. They will pledge and reassure each other of how much they are ready to do in order to sustain their love. This builds very high expectations in each other and as time passes by, they tend to forget the vows. They start resenting each other and sometimes they may sustain the marriages with occasional indulgencies which are not genuine. Gradually, they give up on each other.

Diminished intimacy. As times goes by, it is possible for one partner to simply lose interest in the other or fall out of love especially when children arrive. The mother may get busier and busier with attending to the children and the husband might feel left out. Once their sex routine changes or reduces, the man may decide to seek attention and satisfaction outside the marriage. This is where all excuses will show up such as the wife does not care any more or she has gained too much weight or that she is sulking or she does not take care of herself to look attractive any more.

Another reason under this category could be where sexual intimacy is no longer fun but a routine. If it does not bring pleasure anymore, tension will arise and all sorts of excuses will come up. In some cases a man will just seek his own satisfaction rather than caring how the partner feels. Most women will tell you they never have foreplay. Sex is always mechanical. If a woman feels neglected and used for her partner's satisfaction, she may also seek attention outside her marriage. The outcome will be devastating for both of them and worse for the innocent children involved who have to lose one parent.

Marrying for wrong reasons. An example here would be if either of the partners marries the other for their wealth and not because they love them. When love is not genuine no matter after how long and how many children are already be in the family, if this wealth is lost, love will go with it as well.

However, there are strong cases where a woman might deliberately marry a wealthy man for his money and after a certain period, divorce him so that she can claim his money as in many cases nowadays. In certain countries the law permits the woman and children to have the larger share of family wealth and investments in the event of divorce. If the man is a bad husband or bad father, he is likely to lose his family and everything he has worked for.

Arranged or forced marriages tend not to last leaving mothers with children on their own if love is non-existent.

Other issues that can result in couples splitting are involvement in substance abuse by either of the partner, domestic violence, in most cases caused by the male partner, cruelty, instability resulting from various issues, constant complaints or nagging, family members of either partner, especially in-laws, having a negative influence on their son or daughter living under the same roof and interfering in the marriage issues.

There are cases where couples with children have split after one partner deciding they want to be gay, leaving the other partner to fend for the children.

With all these factors and many more, couples with children are likely to drift apart and end up in divorce, hence one parent becomes custodian of the children involved.

➤ **Teenage Pregnancy**

Most teenage pregnancies are unintentional therefore parents, schools, carers and the governments need to reach out to protect and educate our teens beforehand to protect them from this peril. Research indicates that girls as young as thirteen are likely to fall pregnant once they become sexually active. There is a high tendency of teenage mothers staying unmarried and continuing to give birth to more children out of wedlock. Usually, the fathers responsible for these pregnancies will be young themselves to be responsible fathers, hence abandoning the full care of the babies into the hands of these young and vulnerable mothers.

The most **probable causes of teenage pregnancy** are;
- Lack of sex education such as birth control and safe sex either at home or at school.
- Lack of love, affection and guidance from parents can cause a young girl in the family to seek attention elsewhere in the wrong place.
- Irresponsible parents who expose their sexual behaviors to their children.
- Lack of discipline and irresponsible behavior by teens themselves. Parents need to take action and seriously supervise their children's activities. Children need family values and ground rules to abide by.
- Peer pressure – a desire to be part of the group emulating what their friends are doing.
- The adolescent stage can easily lead a teen to crave for sex naturally but without knowledge of how to deal with it, they find themselves trapped into a series of sexual activities without any control.
- The media - early exposure to sex on television, movies and magazines is a direct attraction to young people.
- Social networking can directly or indirectly link teens to wrong people sometimes.

- Early involvement in alcohol and substance abuse.
- Sexual abuse by irresponsible adult men.
- Women trafficking or sex trade trapping of young women into early motherhood.

According to the Family Planning Association, the UK still has the highest rate of teenage pregnancies compared to the rest of Europe. Findings indicate that the most vulnerable groups likely to become parent teens are those young girls who are still in or are;
- Leaving Care.
- Those who are homeless.
- Those who are underachieving at school.
- Teens from some ethnic minority families.
- Young girls whose parents were also teenage mothers.

Another group identified are those with a history of crime. The surveys showed that a bigger proportion of these groups are the young people living in socially deprived areas where most families are on low income.

Teenage pregnancy is a global concern as not only teens from developing countries are victims, but even those in developed countries.

Surprisingly, it is not as common for teen girls from tropical African countries to fall pregnant as cultural values and restrictions in many families protect them. To some cultures in Africa, sex before marriage is not negotiable, it is a taboo and falling pregnant can lead to heavy punishment and being cast out of the family clan. To date, value is still placed on virgins in some cultures. When girls get married, if a husband finds the young woman not a virgin, they have a right to return them to the parent family. Although this is fading away with modern life styles, men are still particularly serious about it and most parents want the fame of giving away their daughters in formal marriages. Cohabiting is condoned in some areas.

> **Separation of Parents**

Parents can opt to live separate lives having either reached a consensus or it can just happen randomly as a result of a combination of factors similar to those in divorce. They might decide to have a time of reflection away from each other either temporarily so as be able to mend their relationship, or it can be an ultimate base for a divorce. Whichever way, if there are children involved, unless they agree on shared responsibility, one parent will end up the sole provider for everything.

> **Domestic Violence**

Domestic violence is defined as *"Any incident of threatening behaviour, violence or abuse between adults who have been intimate partners or family members, regardless of gender or sexuality."*
Because domestic violence happens inside the home environment, mothers and their children are usually the victims. Domestic violence or spousal abuse is the greatest single catastrophic cause of family breakdown leading to single parenting all over the world. It affects anyone regardless of economic status, ethnic background, age or social status.

Causes of domestic violence
- Distorted mindset of manhood, usually men are the abusers believing they have control over women.
- Controlling behaviour.
- Personality disorders and mental illness.

- Misuse of alcohol and substance abuse.
- Financial insecurity.
- Low self esteem, feeling one partner is doing better than the other.
- Excessive jealousy over the other partner.
- Social stress depending on one's responsibilities.
- Poverty.
- Infidelity.
- Lack of trust in the relationship.

> **Unplanned pregnancy**

It is not only teens that become pregnant unintentionally. Some unmarried adults may also fall pregnant through casual relationships or one night stands without realizing and decide to keep their children. If they do not marry, they will remain single parents.

Desire to have children in the event of delayed marriage. If a woman does not find a partner and yet wishes to have children, she can choose to get pregnant through a casual relationship and look after her own children. Others find surrogate mothers and fathers or decide to adopt.

Likewise, some men who may have had children out of wedlock may decide to keep their children without having to marry the mothers of these children. It is normal for a man to have up to three children from different mothers without marrying them. It may not be acceptable as a cultural practice in some societies, but these children are still innocent and neither should their fathers or mothers be blamed for that.

Spousal Death due to illness or accident or murder.

Rape can result in pregnancy hence making the woman become a single mother.

A parent walking out on the family for various reasons.

A husband or wife can commit a crime and end up in prison leaving one parent to fend for the family.

➢ Isolation Within a Marriage

Although we see many couples together as a family, the truth is that some of them actually live like they are single parents just because they have inside marital issues and feel isolated from each other. Maybe, the husband is always away from home most of the time or even does not contribute to support the family, but he is just there in disguise. It will be the mother fully supporting the family. As a couple, they could even be having separate bedrooms and rarely speak together. Mother feels secluded and children alienated. As a matter of fact, this is no different from any other single parent family. So therefore, we can't significantly take married couples for granted, but just continue praying for all families with marital issues and concerns.

Chapter Three

Myths About Single Parenting

More often, society has labelled black families as the champions of broken families and pioneers of single parenthood rooted from the times of slavery when families were torn apart and parents whisked away from their homes to modern day when they are still discerned as indigent and always marginalised in Western society. Nothing could be further from the truth but who is to blame? Those who invaded African societies and disorganised the family structure or the victims?

Generally, African families in African nations have stable families and the rates of divorce, single parenthood and teenage pregnancy are not as rampant as in Western society. This is due to the fact that historically, most cultures never condoned any of these aspects of life. Divorce or teenage pregnancy or single parenthood were abominable and unheard of. Whether in poverty or wealth, families stick together. If a man has concerns about a wife who is not hardworking, he invites the clan members to sort out the issues and consults the aunties to retrain the woman for motherhood. If not, they agree to return the woman to her parents and ensure she stays there for sometime and learn extra skills then she is taken back. But normally, through rites of passage traditions, young girls are trained to be good wives and mothers and even if the husband misbehaves, they stick to their new family and build their homes. Divorce was unheard of. Men rarely cheat because they do not have that time, they are always busy in charge of household duties or work that earns them income in rural areas. In the cities, a few cases of extra marital affairs can be heard but not common. Yes, things have changed but cases of single motherhood are not rampant.

The single parent adversity is not, however, prevalent in only black parent families but in all families on the face of the earth. Broken families exist everywhere and no one is immune. Causes of divorce and separation and conception are the same everywhere therefore myths about single parenthood are equally the same in every society;
- Single parent homes are regarded as broken, non standard, non-traditional families.
- Children from single parent families are academic failures and have emotional and behavioural problems

- Single parents, especially mothers, are dependent on welfare benefits and all they do is produce more children whom they cannot give a quality life.
- Young offenders especially males are those who are brought up by single mothers because they lack father figures as role models.
- Married mothers always disrespect single mothers and regard them as failures who could not make their marriages work.
- Single mothers cannot afford a holiday, besides they have no savings and are not self-sufficient.
- Single mothers have no time for their children and never give them quality love as do those from married couples.
- Single mothers are failures who cannot contribute positively to their communities because they have no time to interact with other people.
- Single mothers are lonely and miserable and deserve sympathy and pity.
- Single mothers are loose and sleep around with anybody and have less time to supervise their children.
- Single mothers never have enough financially to secure for their children's future.
- Single mothers are incapable of owning a home single handed.

- Children from single parent families have no self esteem and lack confidence in themselves. That they are more likely to drop out of school than other children.
- Most single parents are black families because black males have the highest figure of unemployment, are most irresponsible and low achievers in education.
- Children from single parent families are likely to get involved in gang activities, violent crimes and end up in jail or commit suicide.
- It is also claimed that because of inconsistent disciplining patterns towards children, single mothers are more likely to clash with their older children.

These perceptions may be true to some degree but certain issues of life can never be generalized. Therefore, these myths are just some people's perceptions and can be challenged in many ways with evidence, as already pointed out in this book.

Chapter Four

What Children Need

Every parent would like to fulfill the needs of their children regardless of circumstances. Psychologists of child development indicate that there are specific fundamental needs that every human being requires for survival and these are essentially, the Basic Needs. What are basic needs? These are food, water, shelter, clothing, sanitation, education and healthcare.

These are the essential needs required for personal and social development of a child.

- Healthy and nutritious diet for proper development including air and sleep.

- Every child needs to feel safe and be in stable and secure conditions.

- Every child wants to be loved and have a sense of belonging through the parental relationship.

Chapter Five

Questions to Jog Your Memory - and Get You Started on Something Worthwhile

It is never too late to start all over again. It is never too late to learn and catch up with the rest of the progressive world. Ask God to teach you lessons for living so you can stay the course. Regardless of what you have been through or how many mistakes you may have made. We all have opportunities to think through our experiences and make a decision to try and turn everything around for our own good.

Always look back and reflect on your personal life's journey and where you have come from, where you are now and focus on how far you have to go. Ask yourself if it is worth quitting now or staying where you are while the rest of the world rolls on. Sometimes it is through challenges in our lives that we are able to seek further ways of turning things around for our own good. It is not right to sit back and question all the reasons why you are going through this and that and validating your suffering. Rise and make a move to transform your life.

Life is a classroom in which we learn lessons of all kinds. Right from childhood, through to adolescence and into adulthood, throughout different stages of life, a lot is acquired and absorbed and assimilated and digested. Lessons and experiences which are learned, dropped and forgotten along the way, and others retained all seem to stick with us forever. Do we really ever forget what we go through in life? We perhaps do let go, but we do not forget. We deliberately retain what we need and what we think we don't need, we discard, especially the harsh and most painful experiences, bad memories, disappointments and hurts of all kinds.

Sometimes we seem to be addicted to our memories good or bad, and some thoughts we never let go, they cling on throughout our lives as we nurture them. It is up to you to disregard the odds in your life and follow your instincts. You have to carefully pay attention to your heart and your intuition, in most cases the most painful experiences cannot be easily ignored or forgotten, but you have to choose the best means of healing the pain yourself by dealing with them from the roots.

Some things you can experience but you cannot explain. However, some painful experiences teach us worthwhile lessons as the saying goes, that there is always good in every painful situation. Life becomes the best teacher after we have learnt and mastered the lessons and experiences of life. Do not be afraid to explore, reflect and speak out both the most cherished and the unpleasant memories that you have encountered and believe to have possibly shaped you into the kind of person you are today. History is important as it shapes us into who we are today.

What has life taught you and what have you learnt from each experience?

- What did you learn from your parents as a child?

- What have you learnt from being a parent?

- What have you learnt from being a mother or a father?

- What have learnt from your close family relations?

- What have you learnt from winning?

- What have you learnt from disappointments?

- What have you learnt from betrayal?

- What have you learnt from failure and defeat?
- What have you learnt from your family and friends and other relationships?
- What have you learnt from your personal or faith or spirituality?
- What have you learnt from taking risks or holding back?
- What have you learnt from reaching out to others?
- What have you learnt from waiting?
- What have you learnt from your mentors and teachers?
- What have you learnt from pain whether physical or emotional?
- What have you learnt from your critics?
- What have you learnt from embarrassment and humiliation?
- What have you learnt from setbacks?
- What have you learnt from compromising?
- What have you learned from loving someone who does not seem to love you back?

- What have you learnt from prayer?
- What have you learnt from wasting time?
- What have you learnt from lack of money?
- What have you learnt from having enough money?
- What lessons have you learnt from repeated mistakes?
- What do you think you have leant from meeting the wrong people?
- What have you learnt from meeting honest and reliable people?
- What lessons have you learnt from doubting a situation before making a decision?
- What lessons have you learnt from judging others?
- What have you learnt from being judged?
- What lessons did you learn as a child, as a teen and as an adult about who you are now?
- What lessons have you learnt from procrastination?
- What lessons have you learnt from choosing to be silent or deciding to speak out?

- What lessons do you still need to learn?
- What do you want to change?
- What do you wish you could have changed?
- What regrets do you have now?
- Could things have been different?

Whatever the lesson, whatever the regrets, whatever the successes, whatever the disappointments, whatever the joys, tell your story to build a bridge on which others can walk towards telling their own stories. Maya Angelou, the author of "*Why Caged Birds Sing*" teaches that "*When you learn, teach, when you get, give*".

Grow past your disappointments. Try and be the one to disappoint disappointments by learning every good lesson from them. When you learn from a painful experience, you grow stronger and this enables you to teach others from first hand knowledge. As you teach others, you instantly feel transformed into a new and better you. You are teaching what you have experienced first hand, you have mastered it and you are living the truth of victory. Trials in life enlighten us and shape us into better people. That means you have been tried and tested, like you have been through a refiner's fire, like pure gold. Gold extraction is a long, complex painful process that includes drilling and crushing it into multi stages so the goldsmith can reach the final stage having removed all the impurities. And so is you once you have endured the prime trying, you will be a totally transformed individual ready for any challenge that will show up along your way. You would not want to return to where you have been in the furnace.

The opportunity to learn from your flaws and mistakes and overcome your disappointments is one of the most empowering opportune moments you can ever experience. It is then that we learn that we could have avoided certain situations had we done things differently or moulded our thoughts positively. When you learn a lesson in the midst of adversity, that lesson becomes a lesson for life, it stays with you for life. Learn to appreciate every trial you encounter and learn from it. Learn to see beyond your fears and challenges. There is always light at the end of the tunnel, as the saying goes. Reflect on the valuable parts of your experiences and take more steps to move forward. Keep on keeping on. Aim at improving your life constantly.

"The act of taking the first step is what separates winners from losers"

Brian Tracy

Chapter Six

Common Struggles of Single Parents

Every single parent is aware that all their family responsibilities are upon their shoulders. They have to draw plans of how they will meet their family needs single handedly, whether it is as a working parent, a studying parent or a full time mother at home.

- It is always difficult to have enough time to play all the roles at the same time with no support. For instance, a working parent with school-going children will need to have enough time to prepare them in the morning, ensure they have breakfast and drop them off at school on time and be ready for work. These children will need to be picked up from school or from after school clubs on time and follow the evening routine until bedtime. This can be very tiring to cope with all week.

- Constant responsibilities leave no room for a single parent to balance their own life. There is no time for social activities and relaxation which is not good for a healthy mind.

- Children themselves need to have fun to participate in various activities for healthy growth and development, time to relax and play and socialize with others. At the same time they need all the love and attention to be reassured that they are loved and not feeling like they are a burden to the parent.

- Hiring baby sitters is expensive, childcare is more costly. For those who have a circle of family and friends, they can be of great support.

- A single parent who is juggling between work and studies can find it extremely difficult to study and complete course work at home with younger children who constantly demand attention. She will have no enough time to supervise her children's activities as well.

- Most single parents survive on limited resources with their children. One parent is the sole source of income and the bread winner. If the income is low, the family cannot get enough. They will always have shortage of everything. Financial scarcity is a major concern and normally results in debts which can be a problem to repay.

- Budgeting can be helpful, but that means having enough surplus to sustain the entire family and a handful to put aside for savings. This can be extremely difficult to live within their means.

- Loneliness is a common phenomenon that cannot be denied. Every human being needs a constant companion to talk to, have fun and share problems with. That is crucial as two people can share ideas and come up with solutions to certain issues rather than one.

- If a single parent has children with challenging behaviour, it can be a great concern of how to support these children and they might be taken away into care against the parent's wish.

- Illness of a single parent or children is the most challenging factor. If the parent falls ill, life becomes still as there is no one else to carry on with the home support.

Chapter Seven

Fatherless Boys Raised by Mothers

"If you want to be in your children's memories tomorrow, you have to be in their lives today"
Anonymous

"The greatest gift I ever had came from God and I call Him Dad"
Anonymous

"Every man is rich who has a child to love and guide"
Our Daily Bread

Fatherless boys are the boys simply raised by their mothers single handedly in the absence of their fathers. These boys will grow up looking to their mothers as their heroes and role models. They appreciate their mothers' struggles and commitments to bring them up single handedly. They tend to grow mature at an earlier age than possibly boys who grow up with their fathers because in most cases they find themselves having to be part of their mothers' major decisions and plans as soon as they are old enough to understand issues of life, consequently, their mothers look to them for security. But in all this, every boy wishes his loving Dad was around to see him grow up in his presence and enjoy a close warm relationship with him. They will feel it when he is not there. They miss their fathers most and if not carefully monitored and supported to understand why he is not there, they may become disillusioned and fail to cope with life on their own as young adults and later on as adult men. Boys will need a role model who is a father figure, but if there is no one there for them, the strong ones still successfully make it through. I have spoken to a number of boys I have mentored in schools, and three out of five will honestly tell you that they believe that if their dad was around, life would have been different.

The fact that these boys feel let down and betrayed by their fathers in the case of those who have lost them through failures in relationships with their mothers, they always tend to value their mothers more than anything else in the their world, and will specifically and clearly state that they wish they could marry a woman who is just like their mum in character. Research shows that most young males who commit crimes and end up in jail have no father figures in their families. But to a greater extent, there are single mothers we know very well who have produced and managed to bring up respectful, self-disciplined and decent boys. It all depends on the strength of the single mother and how she is determined to bring up her boys.

Dr.Benjamin Carson, a Professor of Neurosurgery, Oncology, Plastic Surgery and Paediatrics at Johns Hopkins University Hospital, who was also awarded the Presidential Medal of Freedom, the highest civilian award in the United States, by President George W. Bush in 2008, talks well of his own mother who raised him and his brother single handedly after their father left. This did not stop him becoming one of the world's most successful and renowned neurosurgeons.

He himself has had a successful family of his own, a great loving father and husband. I could recount many real role model boys brought up in single parent homes just by their mother like him. I will, in a different chapter of this book give an overview of some of the famous people around the world we know of who have changed the world and yet were brought up by their strong, single mothers single handedly.

Dr. Carson states, in his book *"Think Big"* pg 169 that *"......I admire my mother. Although she did not even have the chance to finish elementary school, married when she was thirteen, and her husband whisked her from her native Tennessee to Detroit. Mother never allowed that to hold her back. She simply used the ability God gave her. For her, at the time when she was almost a non reader, insight came from observing others, asking questions and thinking through the answers"*

His own mother narrates the ordeal she went through after her husband left her and her two sons. The boys were so affected that their grades at school deteriorated considerably, they were always arguing with each other as siblings do, but the whole situation of having to cope without a father around worried her big time so that she almost took her own life which would have left her handsome boys helpless and homeless. However, she always managed to pray to God for help. Slowly, she was managing to bring things together and their grades started rising again due to the effort and ground rules she set for them. She endured the mocking from the neighbors and turned to God for comfort and everything. Dr. Ben Carson gives credit to his special mother and all those selfless individuals who showed up to mentor him and encouraged him to press on in life as they saw much potential in him as a growing teenager.

As a single mother myself raising a boy, there is so much we have had to endure on a daily basis, especially surviving on limited finances and developing my own parenting style while endeavoring to be a perfect and effective parent. I have had to endure certain people's negative perceptions of me and my character and the fact that they think I give too much attention to my boy to the extent that I have no social life. However, I must appreciate that many more people love me and appreciate me for the choices I have made to concentrate on taking care of my son in the midst of almost impossible circumstances. I must confess that I am not the most sociable, outgoing person, I like to get on with my stuff and spend my time reading all kinds of books, but I have met wonderful people whom we get along really well and I am so grateful for all of them.

I see myself as a self-driven and highly ambitious individual who works tirelessly and is always searching for better ways to improve my life. However, like many other people, I have been shaken to the core by certain circumstances such as rejection, being homeless, marriage breakdown, illnesses, insurmountable debts, long time unemployment, betrayal, repeated mistakes, prejudice and all kinds of disappointments, but through God's mercies, I am still here and going strong, more focused than ever and determined to succeed against all odds.

Just having my son in my life gives me such great strength and energy to look forward to another day, expecting things to get better and better because of him. I am pretty sure these challenges are not there to last a life time, in fact, things keep getting better and better by the clock. I have tried my best to work hard to provide for my son. As a good parent, I have tried to be around for him, showing him that I love him, allowing him to be a boy by ensuring he plays the boys' games of his choice but on my advice and supervision.

Boys love action, and a fast paced life. They love adventure, animation, pop music, they like running about, skating, cycling, bowling, snowboarding, water parks, thrilling rides, sports, fast cars and their food. Even as they grow, their interests and love for video games do not tend to fade away like girls. They will start going for the more advanced technology stuff as they get older.

We, as children growing up in the tropics of Africa, were always reminded that that "*Boys were boys*" and I have always found myself letting him be that kind of boy who feels sure and confident of himself. Like most little boys I know, he grew up saying he wants to be a policeman and with so much passion for fast, racing cars, which ardency he has maintained to this day at the age fifteen, but of course that of becoming a policeman has since changed. I believe it is the authority and power these little boys are aware policemen have by the virtue of their duties that makes them admirable and heroic. There were times when he spoke of becoming a pilot so he could fly big planes in the air or being a fireman because they rescue people. He is now a teenager and his most favorite games are still a series of *"Need for Speed"* racing cars and skate games. He loves basketball, snowboarding and cycling with friends on their BMXs. He has fallen off his bike a handful of times trying to do dangerous tricks, but that does not stop him trying again and again. I keep reminding him to ride carefully and avoid the so called *"tricks"*. As polite as he is, he will still say *"Mum I know what I am doing"*. He says after all that's what the fun is all about.

When I remind him to wash the dishes, and ask why he is taking his time. He says that I don't specify the exact time to do something when I ask him to. He points out the fact that I leave loopholes in my statements as he would expect me to say "wash the dishes right now or by this time". It is not disobedience, but he is rather trying to say indirectly that mum you are not always right.

Chapter Eight

Questions That Children Ask: How to Respond

Children of any age are very curious when they realize one of their parents is missing especially their father. Every child wishes to have their father around like other families they meet at school or at church or at parties or in the neighborhood. Fathers are a symbol of pride in the life of a child and an emblem of protection and security to his family. If children are born and find no fathers, they will ask, if he disappears or just walks out on the family in their presence, they will still ask because they want him around if he is a good dad who loves them. They all desire a bonded family. It feels natural for every human being I suppose to be around a real family environment of father, mother and siblings. That's why Christmas comes out to be a very special family time. Everyone comes over and they share their happiest moments together. Nowadays many people are set out to search their long lost family members through the Genealogy, Family Tree and Family History. Family is very important to all of us, whether biological or those who choose to love us as part of their family.

Only the children who have witnessed the abuse of their father towards their mother or have themselves experienced the abuse are likely to understand and be able to accept their single parent family.

So how should single mothers or even single fathers respond to these painful and challenging questions? Do they have to tell the truth? Do they ignore? Do they cover up? How do they deal with it to reassure their inquisitive children? What is the best approach to ensure these children learn and embrace the truth?

Children are innocent in the midst of all these complex marital problems. Regardless of how tense it may be, they will need some proper explanation soon or later for them to understand and be able to move on in life. If there is anybody who is most affected by separation of two parents or a broken home, it's the children who become broken vessels and their wounds can last a lifetime.

As a mother, or even as a single father, if you are the victim, if need be, find professional help so that you are able to find the right answers to reassure your children. They always believe they are the reason behind their parents' break up. Don't let them blame themselves. It will affect their self-esteem and find it hard to cope with difficult situations later in life as adults. Neither should you feel guilty for what has happened. Instead, seek the means to recover and heal from the pains and turn your mess into a message of hope for all concerned. I have gathered a number of questions from some single mothers including those that I have been asked personally by my own son.

Questions frequently asked by children and their statements;

- I wish my dad was here.
- I really miss my dad.
- Who is my dad?
- Where is my dad?
- Do I have a dad?
- Why does my dad not want to stay with us?
- Why does my dad hate me?
- Is it because of me that my dad left us?
- Why does my dad not come to my birthday?
- Why did you separate with my dad?

- Why do you and my dad always fight or yell at each other?
- Why doesn't my dad want to give us money?
- Why are you and my dad not talking to each other?
- Why is my dad living with another woman?
- This is not my dad, why does he stay here?
- How come me and my brother/sister have different dads?
- Is that man my uncle?
- Should I call him my dad?

The list is endless but you need to gracefully and truthfully respond to each question with diligence because the answer you provide or respond with stays with them forever.

Chapter Nine

Single Mothers By Choice

I have spoken to a number of single mothers like myself and asked their views of being single parents. A few of them were honest enough to confess that they wished they were still together with their husbands or fathers of their children. I wish mine too was around for me and my son. Life would have been different and much better. I have also spoken to some single dads and they have their views as well.

However, some parents were able to reveal that they prefer to be independent and look after their children freely with no hustles of manipulation and pain. Essentially, they meant that they would rather live alone instead of being treated like rubbish or nobodies by their partners. Every one's story is different in its own way. I appeal to the world to simply respect single parents and not judge them regardless of who is wrong or who is right. You must listen to both sides before you draw your conclusions and judgements on anyone. The process of loss or break up affects either partner equally. I will mention only two accounts under different contexts.

One particular mother confided in me but permitted me to tell her story as it will be a lesson to some one else. She clearly stated that all she knew about her marriage was like hell. Her and her husband had a grand wedding and a memorable honeymoon. These were to be her last tokens of happiness and most treasured moments. Her beautiful home had become her confinement. Everything changed shortly after their first child. Her and her children constantly lived in fear of their abusive husband and father. He constantly ridiculed her and humilliated her before her growing children. Although he seemed a gentle man, a professional and dignified person to the outside world, a respectful member of his community and church going, he was a monster to his own family. He beat her before she was pregnant. He beat her during her pregnancy that sometimes she thought she thought she would miscarry. He beat her before and after making love to her. He punished and beat her and the children. He beat her after eating a good meal she prepared for him claiming it was nasty and tasteless.

After every beating, he would bring her a bouquet of beautiful flowers the following day and ask for forgiveness. This went on for years. He denied them every privilege in the house. He threw things around and broke plates and glasses and forced them to clean up the mess. He spilled food on the table. He would rape her and burn her beautiful clothes, shoes and handbags. He demanded and kept all the money she earned. No one talked in the house while he was around. Children were never allowed to play about or make noise or even play with toys. He would make these children seat on the floor in the corridor to eat their meals and timed them while they ate, telling them that too much eating will make them stupid.

Whenever they had visitors, he put on a show like he was the best, admirable husband who even helped with the cooking and washing up the dishes. That would be the time he would be seen talking and playing with the three children they had together. He would even buy gifts for the family for Christmas. He dropped and picked the wife from work. He took her shopping and kept all the receipts. He checked and sniffed her underwears just in case she cheated on him. He spanked her for pleasure. He even molested her teen sister who lived with them at one time. He chose for her what to wear. He read her emails and text messages first. He counted pieces of meat they served. They attended church as a happy family and worshipped and praised God. How many couples can relate to this scenario?

He would sometimes drop and pick the children up from school. Ocassionally, they would go out for a meal to an expensive restaurant. She was scared to lose him because she thought and believed that she loved him so much no matter how terrible and dangerous he was. She believed his occassional indulgencies and lived in hope that he would soon change and become a better, loving person. She was scared of the outside world and how she would ever be able to look after her children on her own. She had been told she is damn, stupid and ugly and no one would ever love her. She had confided in her own mother who never believed her. His parents loved him and blamed him for marrying a weaked woman. Who in the world would ever believe her story? She decided to live with it, but for how long? May be it was God's plan. Maybe it was a punishment for her own sins and she was paying back. She was conditioned to this standard default that indeed, she is not good enough and deserves the punishment. He had threatened that should she ever report or tell anyone, he would kill her and her children and no one would ever find them. This is very common in abusive families.

However, she finally had to let the cat out of the bag when she realised the damage this horrendous abuse was causing to her and her children. They had been emotionally, mentally and physically affected. They had developed behavioral and learning difficulties at school. The youngest was diagnosed with autistic spectrum and she could not take it anymore. She found some information on a website in search for freedom. She was ready to risk it or die. She said one last prayer to her God and made her first call in confidence to an unknown person on the other line. For the first time someone listened to her, someone believed her story. Why had she waited all this long? Victims of abuse always believe that things will change for the better soon or later, but it always gets worse. A person who is an abuser in most cases will always be an abuser. It takes more than a miracle to transform them. But there is hope for all. Nothing is impossible with God.

This person on the phone reassured her that it was all confidential. It was a professional and effective response she was looking for at this moment in time or never. She was advised and guided into gathering all the evidence of abuse and then guided her on safety planning to escape. The safety of her children and herself was paramount. For the next few days he could treat her as he wished, but it would not last long after all. God had answered her prayers. Thanks to all such organisations who are there to deliver and support desperate families like Stella's (not her real name).

Eventually, they finally fled the family home in which they had endured so much pain and suffering. They relocated and are now safely and happily living in a secure beautiful home free from abuse. The children can freely play and run about and be children they were never allowed to be. They had been living like caged, abused pets. She has put all these ugly experiences behind her and started afresh. She received quality, professional support and her and her children are going through the healing process by Family Support Groups. The man was apprehended, lost his job and put behind bars for domestic crimes. He would be for parole in nine years. She is now determined to be a great parent and give all she can to bring up her lovely children on her own.

This is one of many similar stories. If the incidents mentioned sound familiar, then you know you are not alone. Learn to forgive and move on with your life. Don't blame yourself for anything. You are a beautiful strong woman who is giving love to your children. Stay positive and believe that God loves you and your lovely children and He wants the best for all of you. Find something worthwhile to do; learn a skill using the existing knowledge and experience you already have, start a small business or something that will earn you some extra income, look after yourself, give the best to your children, they are the reason you are living, choose friends who add value in your life, return to college or university or look for a job you love and move on. You have your whole life a head of you. You have your children to live for.

So, after all, its not always as good as it looks. The ideal family may have their strengths but they also have their own shortcomings. Do not admire or judge anyone you see on the surface if you don't know their inside story. Single parents have their strengths and weaknesses too. Every one has a story behind them. Simply respect other people for who they are and live your own life to the full. I am obliged to say this as I have heard shameful comments and insults hurled towards single parents especially single mothers.

The second account is from a single father of two boys. He reservedly gave his account stating that he still loved his wife so much and his children meant a whole world to him. He however said that he had forgiven his wife of twelve years who walked out on him for another man she had been introduced to by a friend who was happily married. He admitted that he had made mistakes in the past but he was a good provider of his family. He sacrificed and did two jobs to ensure they had everything and his wife was not working. The fact that he spent longer hours working she concluded that he did not give her enough attention and that he must have been having affairs at his workplace. He claimed she had accumulated debts before they met and he had managed to pay them off with his own income. He was now paying the mortgage alone and all other family expenses. She has to support her parents using his money. She still accused him of having affairs of which were baseless. Bruce (not his real name) now feels he is doing very well and giving the best upbringing to his children without being accused of what he is not involved in. He says it will take him a while to trust and love another woman.

"We can never judge the lives of others, because each person knows only their own pain and renunciation. It's one thing to feel that you are on the right path, but it's another to think that yours is the only path"
Paulo Coelho

"We are all stumbling towards the light in varying degrees of grace at any given moment"
Bo Lozoff

Chapter Ten

How Does Single Parenting Affect Children?

All children want to live in a happy, healthy and secure family with mum, dad and sisters and brothers. When one parent is missing, they will ask questions. Where is our mum or where is our dad? The fact that they are ask means they feel the void. Unless they understand that the parent in absence has passed away and non existent, they will keep asking. In this this case, it still takes them a while to recover the loss. Only older kids will understand, but the little ones are likely to ask why their mum or their dad died? They will need to be supported throughout the grieving period and thereafter. Death of a parent leaves a scar on a child forever. Divorce or separation affects children differently depending on age or even gender. It never comes easy on any child to lose a parent.

When marriages or relationships break down and one parent leaves, the children are scarred for life. They feel insecure, alienated and confused. The family upheavals become the children's main concern because they crave for peace and happiness rather than conflicts between their loved parents. They want an explanation because they always think they are to blame for their parents splitting up or fighting. It's the parent's responsibility to ensure children understand why this has happened. In fact they need to hear from both sides so that they don't end up being hateful of the other. Older children can be allowed to be part of the decisions involving their parents' break up.

"A child more than anything would like to move freely between the parents without conflict. They don't want to be pulled into it - they don't want to be a messenger." Marion Stevenson, Oxfordshire Family Mediation,

Children could be allowed the freedom to suggest the arrangements rather than sometimes be forced to stay with a parent they resent. It makes matters worse. If you are the parent with the children, respect the integrity of the parent who has left. Avoid the blame game. Yes, someone may have made mistakes or done something really awful and unacceptable behaviour, but what do you do? You cant live with it, you want to heal from the hurts, pains, disappointments and the irate wounds so that you can move on. Unless you try to forgive and forget and let go, you will be the one to carry the pain throughout your life. The person you may be angry with will move on and will not even remember you exist any more in most cases. Release the grudge and inner strife so that you are free, and peace will always flow through your inner self.

Simply reassure your children that even though things will change or have changed, you still love them as much and you will do your best to be there for them. When they grow up watching how you handle and deal with problems in such situations, they will learn from you when they themselves are confronted with similar challenges in future. I learnt to forgive my own mother having grown up very angry and bitter towards her, why she left us young and vulnerable with our ailing grandmother to return to a neigbouring country. When our grandmother passed away, we all ended up in other people's homes and that was not a pleasant experience for us as children who had had a mother that provided for us and gave us almost everything we needed without lack, yet having no dad in the house.

She was a hardworking, innovative, self sufficient woman who looked after us four children. We came to learn that we had different fathers of whom I never knew who my own one was. Whether this was true or not, it will forever remain a mystery to us.

Such rumours came from people around the village and some relatives.

The man I thought was my father was actually not. He temporarily supported me but it was always a struggle to get what I really wanted as a child for school or other essential needs. I still appreciate the fact that he still managed to do that when he probably knew I was not his biological child. He had only fathered my brother and he fully accepted him and loved him until he joined the army where lost his life fighting for his country. But yet, I was told of two brothers who disappeared while we left one country crossing into the other. My brother I knew left two beautiful girls and his father's family happily took care of them and gave them the love and everything they needed. Our family life remains a mystery to this day.

Separation, family breakdown, death, divorce or even political instability in a country will affect many families and children in different ways;
- They may become withdrawn at school and end up getting bullied.
- Their academic progress may drop to low grades.
- They may hate school and may not look forward to going back home after school.
- Some will develop health issues due to stress especially teens.

- Some of them blame themselves for the family breakdown.
- Others may become resentful to the remaining parent.
- Teens may resort to defiant behaviour such as substance abuse, crime and early relationships to escape the stress and many of them end up in jail at an early age.
- Others may get worried that they are going to lose their home and friends if they move elsewhere.
- Some develop eating disorders.
- Others become bullies at school to divert their anger and frustration.
- Other children become insolent and play truancy.

Some children may strongly survive all the prevailing challenges at the hands of a strong, restrictive single parent, whilst for others their parents may fail to pull through and the negative parenting takes a toll on the children for life.

Chapter Eleven

Starting Another Relationship As a Single Parent

Breaking up of marriages and relationships can be a very terrifying and debilitating experience for those involved. They get apprehensive about the future. They worry about becoming single parents and copying with everything on their own especially when there are children involved. They will also worry about public opinion towards them. This is inevitable and it is natural to feel this way because no one wants to be a single parent at any cost. It is forbidden and unacceptable in most societies. It is a taboo, it is a shameful state of life, though in a normal sense, it should never be viewed this way. In well informed societies nowadays, it is alright to be a single parent.

When you feel as a single parent that you cannot cope on your own, I believe you have a right to make an informed decision and do what you think will make you and your children much happier. Be ready to accept other people as they are, and let them accept you as you are and for who you are. Most people will have close family and friends for support during such difficult times, but others may not have anybody to turn to.

It is very significant once you have decided on what to do after the break up of your family or marital relationship. Ensure you make the right choices especially when you are going through these tough times of disappointments, confusion, discouragement and frustration. When you are feeling hurt, angry and stressed, you can easily choose the easiest way possible to get out of this dilemma, but this is the time to take your time and make more tougher and informed choices so that you may have the positive outcome.

Always remember that there is a higher power, God, in you whom you can rely on to lead and guide you in everything. Even when you don't believe in some kind of spirituality, God Himself still cares for your wellbeing. The book of Hebrews 4:15 states that *"We have a High Priest who understands and sympathises with us in our weaknesses and temptations"*. Ella Wheeler Wilcox teaches us that *"Always continue the climb. It is possible to do whatever you choose if you first get to know who you are and are willing to work with a power that is greater than ourselves to do it."*

Be courageous, be diligent and be wise to follow what is right and compelling for you. Additionally, Donald Trump states that *"As long as you are going to be thinking, think big anyway."*

This is because whatever you are thinking is mostly likely to materialise in the mode you are exactly thinking it. Some times you may be a single parent due to the loss of your partner. Once you have gone through the bereavement and you feel you are ready to start another relationship, it's alright, it's all up to you how you feel about it. You should not let anything hold you back from what you want to do as along as it is the right step foward that will benefit you and your children. You should not be coerced into doing anything unless you strongly feel that is what you want not what you have been asked or advised on to do. However, with children, they need to be consulted and informed of your choices and decisions if they are old enough to understand as they are still going to remain part of your next phase of life.

In most cases, they will embrace the idea because they want to see their mother or father happy again. Take time to think through all the possibilities and challenges this will entail. Consider the fact that your next partner must understand and embrace not just you, but with your children too. Children have to accept this person because if they resent him or her, the relationship will clash and your family will crumble again.

Ask yourself if this person has what it takes to father or mother the children that are not biologically theirs. Most people are of course, and very capable and willing of doing that and happily filling in that gap for the children, but to some degree, there are cases where step parents have turned their step children's lives into living hell. We have heard cases of where blended parents have teamed up to end the lives of their own children so they can be free. God forgive them because that is selfishness of the highest order.

Children are innocent, decent human beings who deserve no suffering of any kind regardless of circumstances under which they are born. They just find themselves born and have no choice to choose where to be born or determine how the circumstances will change. Regardless of the circumstances of their birth, all they require is love and nurturing in the best way possible, until they grow up to be independent.

There are typical instances all over the world we all know of where step fathers have molested their step daughters and vice versa. There are worst cases where fathers have molested their own daughters. This is the most horrifying experience that can happen in the life of an innocent child. Thank God that some children manage to find high quality support and manage to completely recover from their traumas.

Why am I bringing up all these delicate issues? Because you do not want to fall in love with some one who is likely to end up falling in love with your own teen daughter too, or marry a woman who will end up falling in love with your teen son. Actually, they do not even have to be teens. They could be abused at a much tenderer age and by the time you realise it is too late. So, making a choice to remarry or finding a partner while you have children is a very sensitive, delicate and significant decision that must be carefully thought through and involve a strong insight and prayer. Take your time.

Again, believe me, there are incidents where people have prayed for the right partners and believe that these are special, God sent, only to realise too late that they are actually worst than the ones before. So, let us not be carried away by emotions and plunge ourselves into deeper, more dangerous ditches than we have been in before.

Nowadays, you cannot tell who is genuine or not. People disguise under themselves in different ways. Some hide under religion and others will find means of dealing with it as long as they get what they want. Some people are real *"Catfishes"* setting out deliberately to do harm to the innocent. They are up to no good. Some are genuine but they have all sorts of self esteem issues or set out to get revenge, that they think by disguising themselves, they will be able to find partners. Watch the *"Catfish"* documentary by Nev Schulman on MTV based on his personal experience and many others. It is a proper lesson for everyone out there in search of a relationship either for the first time or having a go at a second chance or third chance.

Consider the fact that this person is not marrying you for the wrong reasons as you don't want another break up soon or later. Seek professional advice if you are not sure or simply take time to court the person in order to learn each other. Above all, be led by the spirit of God in you to guide you to the right person through sincere and effective prayer.

If you already have children, are you ready to have more if the new partner wishes to have his own with you too? Have you gathered all the information about his background just in case he or she has already been married and has children from the previous relationship? If this surfaces after you have settled in, will you be able to cope with it? Ensure you talk through all these sensitive matters before you settle down for life.

A genuine prospective partner will open up to you and tell you everything you need to know about them and their history without holding back regardless of how bad or good. Even if they have a spent criminal record, they will be honest with you. Even if they have a hidden disability or disease, they will be honest with you, even if they have been declared bankrupt at some point, they will be honest with you, even if they are fallen heroes, they will be honest with you, if they have divorced, they should be able to open up to you to tell you why their previous marriage did not work so that you accept them as they are and they accept you as you are. Sometimes there are certain things that one may not need to know about a person's history as long as it is not going to affect you in any way, but marriage is a lifetime commitment so things must be revealed honestly. One must be ready to accept you with your baggage and you accept them with their baggage too.

Take Your Time

- Take time to think, It's the source of power.
- Take time to pray, It's the greatest power on earth.
- Take time to play, It's the greatest source of perpetual youth.
- Take time to love and be loved, It's a God given privillege.
- Take time to be friendly, It's the road to happiness.
- Take time to laugh, It's the music of the soul.
- Take time to give, It is too short a day to be selfish.
- Take time to work, It's the source of success.
- Take time to work with love, It is the assurance of success.
- Take time for joyous play, It is the secret of renewing youth.
- Take time to think creatively, It is the foundation of wisdom.
- Take time to love your fellow men, It is the gateway to heaven.

- Take time each day for silence, It is the storehouse of God.
- Take time to worship God, It is the highway of peace.
- Take your time because it is your time.

Author Unknown.

Avoid any habit or things that hinder you from taking time out so that you can live your life to the fullest.

Life is an opportunity, benefit from it.

Life is a beauty, admire it.

Life is a dream, realize it.

Life is a challenge, meet it.

Life is a duty, complete it.

Life is a game, play it.

Life is a promise, fulfill it.

Life is sorrow, overcome it.

Life is a song, sing it.

Life is a struggle, accept it.

Life is a tragedy, confront it.

Life is an adventure, dare it.

Life is luck, make it.

Life is life, fight for it!

Mother Teresa

Chapter Twelve

Blended Families

Blended families refers to two families each with a single parent joing together after a break down or divorce or even the death of one partner to form one complete family. They are also referred to as step families. This can be a new experience for both parents and their children.

Brothers and sisters, mum and dad

Loving each other

Embracing togetherness

New beginnings

Daring start afresh

Enjoying each other's presence

Disciplined and determined to make it work

Many single parents have found true happiness through blended families. One partner may have the children or one child or it can be both of them each coming with their children from a previous relationship or marriage. Sometimes, it can be that one partner will not have children and is willing to have them with this partner who already has, and vise versa. Either way, it can be successfully accomplished and a start of a new beginning.

A good example is one woman from the article in the *Mail On Line* dated 22nd, June, 2009, she narrates her own experience of break up of her formerly happy relationship that left her devastated with one daughter, but she managed to find new love with her childhood sweetheart who had also just broken from his marriage and had a son. When they decided to get back together, she felt this was meant to be. She concludes saying that;

"In an ideal world, it would be wonderful if adults could always be happy with the person they had a child with. But life isn't always like that and our second-best situation seems just as good. Somehow, we've established the perfect family, even if it is a blended and unconventional one"

So therefore, does it matter the background of the family as long as they are happy? single parenthood also should not be taken for granted because things can turn around anytime. Besides, most people find themselves happier and managing well as single parents rather than when they were couples. There is no wrong or right answer.

Chapter Thirteen

Advantages of Children With Two Parents

All children want to have and feel a sense of stability and security in a family home with both parents who are happy too. With each parent having a clearly defined role to support the family in unison, family life becomes delightful and enjoyable for the entire family.

It is believed that a happy family will have siblings who are loving and share everything. They will always get along no matter what challenges that family may face. They stay closely together.

When the family is organised and well structured, children learn their routines, rights and responsibilities at an early age. They become protective of one another and are always self discplined not only in the family home, but portray themselves well outside especially in school and in the community.

They appreciate their parents, family friends and love being identified together because they feel safe, relaxed, happy and comfortable being around each other.

They respect, trust and value each others contributions to the family as they have a strong sense of belonging with a team spirit.

All these characteristics build on to the effective communication that keep the family ties. In difficult times, they tend to encourage and stand for each other.

A happy family shares their spiritual reflections together. They have specific times for family payers and thanksgiving and will treasure that quality time spent together. Each one of them becomes a source of inspiration and will not want to let each other down. Studies in child psychology showed that children brought up in a warm, safe, healthy and happy environment tend to establish strong healthy families themselves as adults because they will have taken examples from their own parents.

This I agree as I have seen certain families closely knit together, bring up their children in the best way possible. These children complete school with no apparent concerns, they fly the nest get jobs and move on to start their own families and follow suit as exactly the families they have been brought in. They carry on the legacy and their family traditions.

Chapter Fourteen

Balancing the Role of Parenting

What do you consider to be your prioritities at the moment? As a parent and single mother or single father, you need to balance your life and ensure that your children are not left out as if they are not loved as much anymore. It could be just one child or four of them or two or eight. They are your children and your priority. Your plans, your goals, your desires, your challenges, your interests, your successes, your happiness, your achievements, all mean everything to them. What affects you, affects them. What affects them, affects you as well. There is an African adage that says *"An elephant can never fail to carry its own trunk."*

However, you must ensure that your trunk does not overload you that you cannot fulfill your roles and responsibilities in every aspect of your life. This will enable you raise a healthy and happier family. Make it all balance.

Which ones of these aspects below would you consider to be your priorities? or are they all equally important? It is imperative that you sit down with your children as a family and discuss your priorities and see how this links in with your responsibilities. Be realistic and work through the list or prepare for any changes and transitions.

PRIORITIES *

Finances

Children's well being

Health

Childrens' education

Quality family time

Relations

Savings

Job

Paying bills

God and faith

Holidays

Social life

Serving your community

* *each reader will prioritise this list according to their own needs and circumstances.*

Deciding on setting priorities that are important to you and your family will help you as a family manage your finances and make informed choices. Consequently, you will be able to set short term or long term goals for the entire family. This is crucial in helping plan your future and what exactly you want to focus on. Make a checklist and keep ticking as you go along. This raises your motivation and energy. Draw action plans and achievable targets especially for the children. Be sure to include everything that matters to you as a family such as above on the list, bearing in mind the SMART Goals. Be consistent in fulfilling the set plans and promises. Increase your momentum and be consistently persistent.

SMART usually stands for:

S – Specific
M – Measurable
A – Attainable
R – Relevant
T – Time-bound

Whatever your goals may be, you will achieve them if you don't give up. Have the patience to continue the journey under any circumstances. Take every obstacle as a learning curve. Do everything with a purpose and integrity.

Connect your goals to your actions

Every action you take today will either move you closer to your chosen goal or farther away from it. There's something you intend to achieve, and the way to achieve it is through action.

There is a very real connection between the things you do and the outcomes you experience. Keep that in mind as you go through the day. Keep that in mind as you decide how to spend your time. Keep that in mind as you control your own thoughts and actions.

Connect your goals to your actions and you will reach those goals. Focus on the outcome of what you're doing, moment by moment. You can choose to just get through the day, or you can decide to make it count and to move yourself forward.

There is a road that runs from where you are right now to the fulfilment of the goals you have chosen. As you go through this day, stay on that road. Keep the connection strong. Take the actions which will move you ahead.

Adapted from Myway Daily Motivator 2013

Family Values

Does your family have specific set values and traditions? These are very significant for every family in that they define who you are and your uniqueness as a family. They create an atmosphere of love, peace, harmony and responsibility to one another. They strengthen family ties and at the same time parental skills and child parent relationships.

Check through these values below and identify which ones are already existing in your family. If not, try and set up some that might suit your family needs with immediate effect. It is never too late although they are always effective when set up right from the beginning. Family values shape the lives and behaviour of children from day one. The moment they are born and find set rules that exist in the family, they will abide and follow suit. Children grow up knowing that for instance, respect and responsibility are not a choice but virtues. They understand that it is for their benefit now and in the time to come when they are adults.

Have a look at some values I have identified on the following page and underline or circle the ones that you think are of interest to you and might fit in with your family.

respect honesty tolerance paid work sense of belonging rights and responsibility discpline loyalty patience generosity sharing family time self control communication education hobbies harmony teamwork budgeting saving volunteering listening to each other love health sharing

A friend of mine was conducting a research on "Student Mothers in Higher Education" for her final year at university, and I happened to be one of her participants. She stated that the research was one of her best learned experiences as she discovered the strength and fortitude these student mothers possess and have had to overcome and the challenges they encounter while studying, working and fulfilling family roles. "It is heroism of its kind" she remarked.

She indicated that the majority of her partcipants were actually single mothers who had to meet all the family obligations and still be there for their childen on top of having to succesffuly complete their varied degrees and graduate, some with first class honours degrees. So, it is possible, after all to set your strategies and priorities and still manage to balance your life. Not as easy but it is achievable. Having set your priorities, stick to family values which will place you ahead of time and strategically guard your motives. She also stated that she realised that there was one common aspect that seems to motivate these participants; that most of them mentioned having specific family values and priorities to adhere to.

What do you consider to be your strength and weaknesses? Once again select from the list on the following pages and circle those that you think apply to you. Then measure them against your own weaknesses and decide how you can work through each of them.

It is always good to understand yourself in order for you to be able to identify where the problems affecting your life are coming from. Once you realize what your weaknesses and strengths are, you can decide to focus on the essential things that need dealing with. For instance, if it is laziness or fear or procrastination holding you back, the moment you recognise them as your obstacles, they will now become your enemies and you will not want anything to do with them. The moment you feel like putting off something that needs urgent action, you will ask yourself whether to go ahead or not. Usually, your conscience will tell you to press on and get it done. You will start to focus on meeting your goals and expectations rather than stay in the old rut that has held you back for years. Move from the old habits, concentrate on transforming your life and enter into a new dimension of your life as a single parent.

STRENGTHS AND WEAKNESSES

Personal Strength	Personal Weakness
Resourceful	Lazy
Success oriented	Quick tempered
Inspiring	Judgemental
Creative	Jealousy
Organised	Procrastination
Determined	Irresponsible
Friendly	Moody
Disciplined	Wasteful
Patient	Arrogant
Persistent	Loner
Optimistic	Shy
Confident	Prejudiced
Self motivated	Bossy
Loyal	Intolerant

Clean	Chaotic
Strategic thinker	Untidy
Open minded	Greedy
Practical	Gossip
Ambitious	Impatient
Tenacious	Rude
Outgoing	Passive
Responsible	Mean
Dependable	Indifferent

Once you analyse your strengths and weaknesses, you can then decide whether you are willing to change your life for the sake of yourself, and your children. Sometimes we are not aware of our human attributes and weaknesses until we are willing to learn. Self awareness and discovery lead to a renewed level of confidence and this will help in shaping the kind of person you become.

Make it a habit to reflect on your positive experiences and which of your strength that could have helped you to be the better person that you are now.

In what situations did you find yourself portraying positive attitude or negative attitude? Think about certain aspects of your life where you acted courageously, showed determination, sacrificed your time or money, showed love to someone, shared anything and being selfless or kindness.

How would other people describe you? *Trustworthy, reliable, sociable, patient, caring, unreliable and untrustworthy, likeable, funloving, cheerful, smiling, helpful* or otherwise?

Can you think of certain areas in your life you would like to change that will make you a better person or better parent?

Are you confident enough that there are certain areas of your personality that your children or other people can always make a reference to and identify with?

Do you still inhibit feelings or emotions of anger, disappointment, regrets, revenge, hateful, fear or sadness?

Are there issues that you feel you need to deal with? Are they to do with your childhood, your upbringing, or previous relationships as a child or later in life as an adult?

Do you think there are still obstacles that are hindering you from reaching your goals in life especially as a parent?

Be Encouraged.

- The future belongs to those who believe in the beauty of their dreams.
- Enjoy life, this is not a rehearsal. Think highly of yourself because the world takes you at your own estimate.
- Do not fear pressure, for pressure is what turns rough stones into diamonds.
- Live each day in the present and make it beautiful.
- Be encouraged that life is worth living and your beliefs will create the fact.
- Wherever you go, take your whole heart along.
- If you love life, life will love you back.
- Heal the past, live the present and dream the future.
- Do not count the days, make the days count.
- The key to happiness is having dreams come true.

- The world is like a mirror, if you face it smiling, it smiles back.

- Happiness is not having what you want, it is wanting what you have.

- Learn to listen, opportunity sometimes knocks very softly.

- Life would be infinitely happier if we could only be born at the age of eighty and gradually approach eighteen.

- Good times become good memories, bad times become lessons.

- It is not only the scenery you miss by going too fast.

- Success is to get what you want, luck is to keep what you get.

- I look to the future because that is where I am going to spend the rest of my life.

- People are lonely because they build walls around them instead of bridges.

*www.authorstream.com/**Present**ation/Mica-109669-**learn**-**live***

Eleven Hints for Life

It hurts to love someone and not be loved in return. But what is more painful is to love someone and never find the courage to let that person know how you feel.

A sad thing in life is when you meet someone who means a lot to you, only to find out in the end that it was never meant to be and you just have to let go.

The best kind of friend is the kind you can sit on a porch swing with, never say a word, and then walk away feeling like it was the best conversation you've ever had.

It's true that we don't know what we've got until we lose it, but it's also true that we don't know what we've been missing until it arrives.

It takes only a minute to get a crush on someone, an hour to like someone, and a day to love someone - but it takes a lifetime to forget someone.

Don't go for looks, they can deceive. Don't go for wealth, even that fades away. Go for someone who makes you smile because it takes only a smile to make a dark day seem bright.

Dream what you want to dream, go where you want to go, be what you want to be. Because you have only one life and one chance to do all the things you want to do.

Always put yourself in the other's shoes. If you feel that it hurts you, it probably hurts the person too.

A careless word may kindle strife. A cruel word may wreck a life. A timely word may level stress. But a loving word may heal and bless.

The happiest of people don't necessarily have the best of everything they just make the most of everything that comes along their way.

Love begins with a smile, grows with a kiss, end with a tear. When you were born, you were crying and everyone around you was smiling. Live your life so that when you die, you're the one smiling and everyone around you is crying.

Author Unknown

Chapter Fifteen

Single Parent Statistics

Britain

According to the Telegraph newspaper dated Friday, 1st February 2013, it is estimated that the number of single parent families has hit the staggering figure of up to 2 million. *Article by Martin Beckford, Social Affairs Editor 20 Jan 2012. The article indicates that there are more children living in single parent families rather than with married couples.*

- *Some 8,000 same-sex couples now have children according to the office of National Statistics.*
- *4.5 million families in 2011 had children under 16.*
- *Article indicated that although "married couples are still the most common family type", their number is declining as more relationships break down and fewer couples choose to wed.*
- *That between 2001 and 2011, with 62 per cent of children now living with married parents, 14 per cent with cohabiting*

couples and 24 per cent with a single parent.
- *That the number of lone parents with children has risen "steadily but significantly" from 1.7 million to 1.96 million, rounded up to 2 million by the ONS (Office of National Statistics)*
- *That almost all (92 per cent) of these single parents were women: "Women are more likely to take the main caring responsibilities for any children when relationships break down, and therefore become lone parents."*

Source:
http://www.telegraph.co.uk/women/mother-tongue/9025234/Single-parent-families-reach-two-million.html

On the other hand, the Mail Online dated Friday, 1st February 2013 under the article by *Daniel Martin (3rd, August 2012),* shows that single parent families outnumber couple families. Also that *"Britain has highest proportion of single parent families in Europe."*

'Research shows children growing up in fatherless homes are much less likely to do well at school and are at twice the risk of getting into problems with drink or drugs, or involved in crime. The UK welfare system has been partly to blame, by providing a substitute breadwinner rather than encouraging parents to stick together.'

The study revealed that 23 per cent of British children up to the age of 14 live in single-parent families, behind the US on 26 per cent. And 48 per cent of single mothers in Britain are unemployed, the highest rate in the OECD apart from Turkey.

Source:
http://www.dailymail.co.uk/news/article-2183462/Single-parent-families-common-todays-Britain-couples-minority.

UK may have the highest statistics for single parents, but I applaud it as a nation for the responsibility they place upon trying to protect the rights of children, taking care of them and ensuring that the nation's children are secure and safe. For years the country gives priority to looking after single parents with children through the support of their welfare system.

Like many other nations, they have examples of great men who have been brought up by single parents and they are not ashamed to say so. One of them Alan Johnson, who has been a cabinet minister and Home Secretary mentions his ordeal in his recently published book entitled *"This Boy; a Memoir of Childhood"*. He was brought up single-handedly by his working class mother in North Kensington after his dad ran away with a barmaid. To Alan, he more dreaded having a father around than not having one, and by the time he was thirteen, his mum passed away aged forty two leaving Alan and his older sister Linda to fend for themselves. To me, it must have been God who took over the responsibility for whatever they went through after that, to the time he was able to make his way into a ministerial post. There is a lot to learn from such a great example.

This plus so many examples not mentioned here portray a great example for all single mothers out there and their children that nothing is impossible. Your children can leap to great heights in life if they are well brought up and taught the values of life regardless of whether they have a father around or not.

Not only Alan Johnson, but Jack Straw, who has led many top posts in the Labour government, was brought up solely by his mother on a council estate in Essex after his father left the family. This did not deter him from completing school and entering university and going on to becoming one of the exemplary leaders of our time. From

Shadow Cabinet minister, to Home Secretary, to Foreign Secretary, to the leader of the House of Commons and Lord Chancellor. What can any one say therefore that single mothers are failures or that children from these single parent homes are academic failures.

It is believed that a woman cannot raise a strong and brave boy as this child will always be a mother's boy and can never grow up to be emotionally and physically strong. They claim that these boys will have a low self esteem and lack confidence in their own abilities. However, this is not the case.

Chapter Sixteen

Single Parenting Quotes

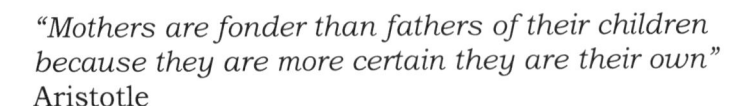

"Mothers are fonder than fathers of their children because they are more certain they are their own"
Aristotle

"Only mothers can think of the future - because they give birth to it in their children"
Maxim Gorky

"Being a full-time mother is one of the highest salaried jobs in my field, since the payment is pure love"
Mildred B. Vermont

"Mothers hold their children's hands for a short while, but their hearts forever"
Anonymous

"Your children need your presence more than your presents"
Jesse Jackson

"Raising a family is difficult enough. But it's even more difficult for single parents struggling to make ends meet. They don't need more obstacles. They need more opportunities"
Bill Richardson

"When you are a mother, you are never really alone in your thoughts. A mother always has to think twice, once for herself and once for her child"
Sophia Loren

"God could not be everywhere, and therefore he made mothers"
Rudyard Kipling

*"I know I am not perfect
And I don't live to be
But before you start pointing fingers
Make sure your hands are clean"*
Bob Marley

They say never date a woman with kids, but nothing is more attractive than seeing a single mother who is in school full time, got two or three jobs, and doing whatever it is possible so her kids can have the best.
NaQuin Gray

Disadvantages of Single Parenting. Are there advantages of Single Parenting?

Some of the single mothers I have personally spoken to have different responses and views towards this question;

- One single mother of two told me that she can only cook whatever she likes at any time for her and her children without anyone despising her or giving her orders what to cook and not what to cook. That if they choose to eat a kebab or pizza for dinner it's fine with them as long as they are all happy.
- On the other hand, one single dad of three when asked the above question responded by telling me that he and his partner were always at loggerheads for

her not cooking because she wanted to buy chocolate, chips, pizzas and fizzy drinks for the children all the time. Every time she attempted cooking, the food would burn or it wouldn't be properly cooked. Since their separation, he had to learn cookery and preparing healthy meals for his children and now they all sit at dinner table and enjoy delicious healthy meals. He also claimed that she had no time for the children, she was always shouting at them, never had time to clean them or clean the house, that sometimes they would sleep in their uniform and go to school in the morning with no proper breakfast. They were unkempt as he was busy working. Reports from school indicated that the children were not taught personal hygiene. This was a big concern as it seems they were like neglected children with no parents. The father decided he had to reduce on his workload to attend to them.

- Another single mother of two teenage boys stated that for years she had to put up with domestic violence and never disclosed it to anybody, not even her own family until she divorced her husband when their children were eight and five. She said she had had enough negative criticism and mental torture. She had no freedom and felt like a slave in her own home. Now she has all the freedom, she has made friends and her and her children are happier than ever. There is no more fear in their home, they enjoy the independence and she can wisely take charge of her finances, budget her own expenses and save for her children. Her children's behavior and performance in school have since improved and she has a good relationship with them.

- You can go wherever you want, as long as you and your children are safe. No arguments, spend quality time with your children.

Despite all the negative factors surrounding the concept of single motherhood, it is evident that to a large extent, after the family breakdown, there may develop an increased sense of responsibility from the remaining parent. She becomes aware that everything is now under her shoulder to bear. Children benefit and enjoy more liberally from this increased level of responsibility.

The Telegraph Monday 28 January 2013
"Children in single parent families 'worse behaved"

Children raised by single mothers are twice as likely to misbehave as those born into traditional two-parent families, according to research"

There are now nearly two million single parent families in Britain, official figures revealed yesterday.

The vast majority are headed by a mother, meaning that millions of children are being raised in households where there is no father.

The figures, from the Office for National Statistics, showed that more than one in four families – 26 per cent – are now led by a single parent.

Ninety-two per cent of single parents are female, and Britain has more single parent families than anywhere else in Europe

Britain is the European leader when it comes to children being raised by just one parent.

Children who grow up in one-parent homes are more likely to suffer poor health, do badly at school and fall into crime or drug abuse when they are teenagers.

The latest figures show that the number of single parent families with dependent children in the UK went up from 1,745,000 in 2001 to 1,958,000 last year.

'We are far ahead of European countries. Single parent families are nearly always led by a mother. Millions of children are missing the experience of having a committed father.'

Tuesday, 29 March 2011

Chapter Seventeen

Famous People Raised by Single Mothers

I came across this dated list from the website below and I thought this was a useful list to look at. Countless people have made it through the hands of their single mothers and credit goes to all of them.

President Barack Obama (met his father only once)

Tom Cruise (he and his 3 siblings were raised by his mother)

Bill Clinton (father died in a car accident 3 months before his birth)

Bill Cosby

Michael Phelps

Demi Moore (father abandoned her before she was born)

Angelina Jolie

Julia Roberts (lost her father when she was 10)

Oprah Winfrey

Aubrey Hepburn

Maria Carey

Matt Damon

Halle Berry (abandoned by her father when she was 4)

Jodie Foster (parents separated before she was born)

Alicia Keys (grew up without her father)

Al Pacino (grew up in his grandparents' house with his mother)

Marilyn Monroe (grew up with no father)

Barbra Streisand (lost her father when she was 2)

Jack Nicholson (did not know his real father)

Pierce Brosnan (abandoned by his father before his 1st birthday)

Jonathan Rhys Meyers (parent separated when he was 3)

Justin Bieber (his mother was 18 when she had him)

Ryan Gosling

Lance Armstrong

Samuel L Jackson (met his father twice in his life)

Jay-Z (abandoned by his father)

John Lennon (grew up with no father)

Charlize Theron (father was abusive and an alcoholic, mother ended up killing him)

Shania Twain

Kanye West

Mary J. Blige (father left when she was 4)

Adele (father left when she was 3)

Online Help For Single Parents

If you are a single mum or dad and you are reading this book. If you have concerns over your parenting skills or children's behavior or emotional issues, visit the following websites for support.

Single Parents / Parental Rights
- *Cafcass.gov.uk - Looking after the interests of children involved in family proceedings*
- *Fatherhood Institute.org - Promoting a society that gives all children a strong and positive relationship with their father*
- *Fathers 4 Justice.org - Campaigning for a child's right to see both parents and grandparents*
- *Fathers for Equal Rights*
- *Fathers for Equal Rights (US)*
- *NACSA.co.uk - UK child support advice*
- *One Parent Families/Gingerbread - Charity promoting lone parents welfare and independence*
- *OnlyDads.org - Support for lone fathers*
- *OnlyMums.org - Help and support for lone mothers*
- *Single Mothers By Choice.com*
- *Single Mothers.org - National Organization of Single Mothers (US)*
- *Single Parents.org.uk - Online community for single parents*

Not everyone views a single parent with a negative perception. There are more understanding people around the world who will accept single parents and love and support them in every way possible. When I was ill one time a few years ago, my church members offered to drop and pick my son up from school. He was in primary school then. They took turns to prepare meals for us and others cleaned our house. That was very kind of them.

Where we just moved recently, our good next door neighbour must have noticed that my son and I do our lawn and fence on our own. So he offered to lend us his equipment to use, and even offered to get his ladders and help us trim the fence. How kind is that. We are grateful to him and his wife. Its like they are always checking that we are ok and safe.

I have struggled for a while finding a steady, reliable employment since graduating from university and I thought to myself that I could actually put to use my skills, knowledge and personal experiences by documenting my thoughts. Then I could write books that will reach out to someone else out there with similar struggles so they know they are not alone. I would love to hear from the readers of this book and would like to hear of their experiences, struggles and joys in being a single parent. You can contact me on this email address: julie.jayson2013@gmail.com

Proclaim God's Word

I will seek justice and encourage the oppressed. I will defend the cause of the fatherless and plead the case of the widow.

Isaiah 1:17

[Scripture personalised by Derek Prince in his book "*Who cares for Orphans, Widows, the Poor and Oppressed... God Does... Do We?*"]